A Primer for
Medical risk management

Dr. Myron M. Persoff, M.D., F.A.C.S.

TABLE OF CONTENTS

Preface and Acknowledgments	01		
The Malpractice Problem	02		
Introduction	03		
Risk Management		Chapter	1
Physician-Patient Contract		Chapter	2
Customer Relations		Chapter	3
Informed Consent		Chapter	4
Medical Records		Chapter	5
Malpractice Hazards in the Office		Chapter	6
The Anatomy of a Malpractice Suit		Chapter	7
Bibliography			
Glossary			
Examination Risk Management Course			

01 PREFACE AND ACKNOWLEDGMENTS

I was a practicing physician, a plastic surgeon in South Florida - the hotbed of malpractice. I had no particular interest in risk management until I got sued for a recognized complication of a cosmetic operation. While I was exonerated of malpractice at the trial, the patient was awarded considerable damages because of the second count of the suit: "lack of informed consent". Despite the fact that the patient had seen one of my colleagues two weeks prior to seeing me and he had "scared her out of the operation", the patient begged me to "spare her the gory details" (which I did), she prevailed in court. Little things hurt my case such as a slight deviation from my usual practice norm -- I allowed her to be "too busy" to come in for a second visit prior to the operation. Also, I didn't document enough in the office records; I failed to get a "receipt" for educational material that I gave to her; and the list goes on. I wanted to learn from my mistakes so that it wouldn't happen again (hopefully). That process helped me to put together this home study course. I truly hope that it serves you well.

Myron M. Persoff, M.D., F.A.C.S.

02   THE MALPRACTICE PROBLEM

The so-called malpractice crisis has been with us since the early 1970's when there was a crisis of availability of insurance. As we moved into the 1980's, the problem became less one of availability and more one of affordability, despite all attempts at tort reform. It was pointed out by one doctor that a malpractice insurance policy for an obstetrician-gynecologist purchased in 1954 with policy limits of $100,000 and $300,000 was $103 per year. The same policy for the same limits in 1985 would cost $200,000 in the same state with no history of litigation and no change in the type of practice.

Many reasons have been sought for the so-called malpractice crisis. A study by the GAO has suggested the following three elements are all somewhat to blame:

1.   The bad doctor. It is generally recognized that not all doctors are of the same quality. Just as in any other profession, there is a bell-shaped curve with regard to ability; however, interestingly enough, only a small percentage of doctors are chronic or repeat offenders with regard to malpractice. It has been shown that possibly three to five percent of the doctor population is responsible for nearly 30% of the lawsuits; however, the malpractice problem cannot be solely attributed to "bad doctors".

2.   The lawyers. While it is true that we live in an increasingly litigious society, and it is also true that many frivolous lawsuits have been brought against physicians, many legitimate lawsuits have found their way into court also. There is an overabundance of lawyers in the United States today. Coupled with an increasingly litigious society, this at least accounts for another of the reasons for the malpractice crisis.

3.   Insurance companies. The GAO has found that while insurance companies have profited from the malpractice problems, it is not true according to their figures that they have profited from the malpractice line any more than from other lines of insurance. Also, physician mutuals, and risk retention groups experience the same problems as commercial companies with regard to adequacy of rates, underwriting, and payout of claims. Truly, the problem is, and will continue to be, multi-factorial.

Yes, it's about the money! When we think about the current malpractice quagmire, it is easy to believe that it is an extremely complicated issue. It is not. It is all about the money. In a perfect world, the problems and complications which occasionally arise in the (usually normal) course of medical care and treatment would be handled with dispatch, first having an open and non-hostile environment for the medical caregivers to minimize the ill-effects of treatment and secondly an economic system to fairly and rapidly compensate the injured patient to cover lost (economic damages) money caused by the medical misadventure. This would be much like the Worker's Compensation schedules or "No-Fault" auto insurance. It would involve a case review by a panel of medical experts to determine if the facts show medical negligence or misadventure. If true negligence is found, the case would be recommended for trial. What do we have instead? A system that is hostile to all, secretive with almost no ability for caregivers to share information for fear of that information ending up in the hands of lawyers. This system does NOT fairly compensate the greater number of injured patients, but sets them into a dizzying tug-of-war between their zealous lawyers (out to right the wronged) and the medical establishment, now on the defensive rather than on the patient's side. Several billion dollars are spent each year in the US on malpractice premiums – money that is no longer going into research or learning. Doctors are no longer free to discuss medical problems and root causes. There are no longer any hospital sponsored "Mortality and Morbidity" conferences for doctors to discuss medical problems and to try to do better. It is almost as if medicine is a forbidden art, being practiced in caves for fear of being found out – and perhaps soon it *will* be illegal to practice medicine, judging from all of the punitive laws that are being levied against the medical community. While I would not argue that some mistakes are definitely the result of exceptionally poor judgment or "malpractice", the very term "malpractice" is an anathema to the practice of medicine. Even the worst practitioner has the patient's best interest foremost in his mind and none of us wakes up in the morning looking forward to killing or maiming someone – quite the opposite. We enter and stay in this field, enduring years of schooling and tough residency training because of altruism, and yes, the money – like everyone else, doctors work for a living.

What does this system do? 55% of the lawsuits filed are dismissed with no payment at all, about 30% reach a pre-trial settlement, and of the remaining 15% that do go to trial, only 38% are victorious – and, boy are they victorious! In Florida, the average court award is now over $2 Million!! In this system, the plaintiff's lawyers walk away with more than 40% of the award when costs are included.   And, the whole debacle takes an average of five years from injury to award.   I ask you, is this a sane system?

Physicians have battled the war for tort reform for over 50 years now with little notice until recently.   The cost of practicing medicine is now in many cases more than the income.   Doctors are going broke.   They are leaving the state or quitting early, or are ceasing to perform "risky" procedures.   Hospitals, birthing centers, and trauma centers are shutting down.   The politicians are just now taking notice – because they perceive that this crisis MAY cause a major disruption in the delivery of medical care.   Our country is known around the world for its "cutting edge" medical care delivery system.   People travel here from all over the world to receive our care.   Is it possible that in this "best of medical worlds" that the majority of the physicians are mal-practitioners?   In California, where the Medical Incident Compensation Act (MICRA) was passed over 50 years ago, premiums have risen 150% in the past 20 years.   In the US, outside of California, the escalation is over 500%, and here, in Florida, over $2000%!!   Is this about malpractice or money?

The lawyers are quick to defend the "contingency fee" system as the poor man's "key to the courthouse".   Strangely, this is the only country in the world with a contingency fee. In other countries, the loser pays all costs.   Here in the U.S., with the current managed care contracts and arbitrary denials of coverage, doctors are doing "pro bono" work even for patients of means.   If the lawyers so strongly believe in their cause they should abandon the contingency fee and be paid for their time like every other working person in the country.

And what about the insurance companies?   Yes, they are also in it to make money. But, when they lose, they lose big!   If their rates are too low in order to be competitive, if underwriting is too lax, if return on investment is less than anticipated for the claims reserve and capital accounts, AND they get hit with higher than expected awards from runaway juries, they, too can lose money and go broke.

I could quote more dull and boring statistics, but the point is just this: The biggest problem facing us today in the delivery of healthcare and its future availability is MONEY.

Managed care has driven physician reimbursements down, while costs to the patients and the taxpayers have skyrocketed. For all this incredible genius, the CEO's of these companies are making multimillion-dollar salaries. A relatively few injured patients are becoming "instant multimillionaires" while other injured persons languish. Many lawyers are now able to purchase small countries with the enormous sums garnished by contingency fees – all in the name of helping humanity.

Do we need tort reform? You bet! Without it, medical tourism will be reversing directions _from the US_ to get better and cheaper medical care in foreign hospitals! Locations like Mexico, South America, Thailand, China, have no medical liability crisis and the cost of medical care is low as a result. But the quality of care?

03 INTRODUCTION:

As practicing physicians, we find ourselves faced with a dilemma not taught to us in medical school. As physicians, we are, by our very nature, humanists. We do not believe that one patient needs to be sacrificed so that another may live, but in the adversarial practice of law, there is only one victor and one vanquished in a dispute. (In reality, BOTH parties lose and the lawyers win.) We have been taught to do our "very best" and accept the consequences when that falls short of the mark.

However, a new consumer spirit has arisen in America and often, "our very best" is simply not enough. Our forefathers in medicine were considered heroes when all they could do was to hold a dying patient's hand (a patient dying for the lack of modern medical expertise). We, on the other hand, are sometimes thought of as villains even when we have successfully defeated the ravages of Nature, stamped out disease, defeated death and disability, and made triumphant progress with the use of new medical technologies and techniques.

Perhaps what is missing is that the nurturing and handholding physician is now an anachronism, replaced by the physician-technocrat. Understand, however, this is not said as an indictment, but merely an observation of what could be causing the total phenomenon that is now occurring. Unfortunately, we cannot go back to the "good old days."

Malpractice suits have become a way of life in the United States and the causes are not too clear for those of us who daily practice "in the trenches." We have heard of the twenty percent of malefactors who are supposedly responsible for the majority of suits. However, if we look at the number of physicians sued and the profile of these physicians, we discover that most of them are not the malefactors, but simply good practicing physicians, who have either taken on too great a challenge, suffered the "slings and arrows of outrageous misfortune", or simply practiced long enough for the odds to catch up with them.

With this in mind, we have put together this risk management course in an attempt to teach some basic facts about the development of a lawsuit and its possible prevention, i.e., to develop the skills required to avoid a malpractice claim. These are facts which have not, to date, been taught in medical schools, but hopefully one day will; lessons which must be learned in order to continue to practice medicine and not law. Consider this: the proper steps taken during treatment will win a case far more easily and less expensively than the cleverest defense attorney. What is the cause of the *malpractice crisis?* Many will blame the doctors and an equal number will blame the lawyers. Some blame society and others the insurance companies. The real answer is probably a combination of all. There are both bad doctors and lawyers. Our society is increasingly litigious and it is a proven fact that the insurance industry, per se, has been less than totally honest with physicians concerning premium increases and actual losses. It is now our task to try to utilize those lessons learned in court and through long experience to teach our members a rational method of prevention of lawsuits. This will help you prevent potential suits as well as better prepare you to win if sued.

1 RISK MANAGEMENT

Definition As it pertains to physicians, risk management is the technique of utilizing communicative skills combined with proper chart documentation to minimize the possibility of a successful lawsuit against you for medical malpractice. Two key words are important here:

1. "Minimize" implies that utilizing the techniques of risk management may prevent the actual filing of a lawsuit.

2. "Successful" implies that utilizing proper documentation techniques will (hopefully) render a verdict in your favor if a lawsuit is filed and goes to trial.

The legal system operates with words. As physicians, we do not realize the importance of words or, more importantly, the effect or lack of effect, of them on our charts to show the reasonableness of treatment, when the outcome is adverse and a malpractice action is tried in court. It is often not reason that prevails. As previously stated, we physicians are trained to follow wisdom and reason; however, as it pertains to law, we must learn that while law is based on a "search for the truth", verdicts are seldom rendered on the basis of truth, but rather on a successful presentation by the lawyer of his or her version of the truth which, parenthetically, may have nothing at all to do with the medical facts. This should not serve to make us cynical, but rather forewarn us of the absolute necessity for proper documentation so that you can aid your attorney in presenting your version of the truth. A well documented chart provides proof of your medical plan and the patient's reaction to therapy. Ina war of words, documentation is both the armor and the ammunition.

In today's medico-legal climate, the wise physician not only (1) dispenses good medicine in a competent fashion, but also (2) establishes good rapport with his patient. Further, he is (3) able to adequately document everything in the course of treatment from the initial consultation to the last office visit. While we hate to think of the practice of medicine as adversarial, a court of law certainly is. The following charge by a judge to a jury is elemental for the understanding of the problems we face:

> *"A physician and surgeon, by taking charge of a case, implicitly represents that he possesses the case. The law places upon him the duty of possessing that reasonable degree of knowledge and skill ordinarily possessed by physicians and surgeons, in the locality where he practices, and which is ordinarily regarded by those conversant with employment as necessary to qualify him to engage in the business of practicing medicine and surgery. Upon consenting to treat, it becomes his duty to use reasonable care and diligence in the exercise of his skill and the application of his knowledge to accomplish diligence in the exercise of his skill and the application of his knowledge to accomplish the purpose for which he was employed. He is under obligation to use his best judgment in exercising his skill and training. The law holds him liable for an injury to his patient resulting from want of the requisite knowledge and skill, or the omission to exercise reasonable care, or the failure to use his best judgement."*[2]

This charge to a jury could have as easily been written today as it was in 1898. In essence, it states that we must use reasonable care and diligence and are not required to be extraordinary in order to practice good medicine. We are expected to practice the same way as the average member of the medical profession in good standing. However, a mere error in judgment would be acceptable, provided that this error was made after careful examination and thought.

Then, WHAT IS **RISK MANAGEMENT**? It is, primarily the use of hindsight to develop clear foresight so as to prevent recurrences of problems through:

1. Identification of risk,
2. Control of risk, and
3. Prevention of risk.

WHAT IS MEDICAL MALPRACTICE? Legally, medical malpractice requires three basic elements:

1. The existence of a valid physician-patient relationship or contract for services,
2. Negligence or fault in the carrying out, or providing of medical care, and
3. Injury to the plaintiff (patient), which is the direct result of the negligence.

In simpler words, medical malpractice is negligence by a physician or his agent in the care of a patient, which has been the direct or proximate cause of injury or death.

WHAT IS PROXIMATE CAUSE? This legal term means that a course of action (or inaction) without any material intervention has:

1. Caused the untoward result, or
2. Precipitated the condition, or
3. Aggravated the condition.

Many factors are involved in the increase of malpractice litigation. One already alluded to is the lack of intimacy in today's Doctor-Patient Relationship. With this somewhat less intimate situation, the doctor becomes more or less a third party (often as a consultant, "referral", or as a Director of the medical technology applied for the patients' benefit.) This has caused the doctor to be somewhat of a stranger to the patient. This is especially true in services such as Anesthesia, Emergency Medicine, and consultative services such as Hematology, Pathology, Radiology, and the like. These doctors are, for the most part, unknown to the patient even though they may have done an adequate job in performing their duties. When things go wrong, it is easier to attack an unknown person compared to the old hand-holding "doctor friendly" of the past. Another contributing factor is the development of *great expectations* on the part of the patient population at large engendered by constant media exposure of modern medical miracles such as organ and limb transplantation, genetic manipulation, modern pharmaceuticals and so on. When the result of a loved one's care falls short of perfection, the tendency is to blame the physician.

America is known to the world as "Sue City" as we are the most litigious society on the planet. Everyday, newspapers bombard us with the results of lawsuits, often being brought for exceedingly unusual reasons, and some bordering on the ridiculous. The advertisement of jury verdicts in the millions of dollars also feeds the *lottery mentality*. Finally, and perhaps most importantly, people sue because they are angry! An unusually high medical bill may have surprised them; they may have had a major disagreement with the physician; or, they may simply have come upon bad economic circumstances. Couple this with an unexpected outcome, high hopes, and visions of millions of dollars being awarded, and you have the makings of a lawsuit!

MALPRACTICE INSURANCE PRIMER

Many physicians have only a vague understanding of malpractice insurance with regard to the different types of policies available, limits, etc. Essentially, there are only two types of insurance available -- occurrence and claims-made.

1. OCCURRENCE: This is the truest type of insurance whereby anything that "occurs" during the policy period is covered. That is to say, that every act within the time the policy is in force is covered no matter when the claim is made. It is the more ideal type of insurance, but is much more expensive and generally unavailable today. Once the premium is paid, any and all claims arising from activities in the year(s) the policy is in force are covered until the statute of limitations for claims runs out. This coverage will still be in effect after the death of a physician covered by an occurrence policy (assuming, of course, that the insurance company is still viable).

2. CLAIMS-MADE: With this type of insurance, the insured is covered only for claims which arise during the period of time the policy is in effect; that is to say, if the occurrence is during the policy period, but the claim is made after the policy period lapses, then no coverage exists unless the insured has purchased additional insurance called a "tail". The tail coverage is usually very expensive; often three times the cost of the first year's premium. Claims-made insurance is more popular because of its low front-end cost. It is predicated upon the following premise: During the first year of the policy, the chances of a claim arising from actions of that year are quite small, but the chances increase each year until year five, at which time the policy is considered a "mature claims-made" policy, and the premium approaches that of an occurrence policy. In fact, the discount over an occurrence policy after five years is only between five and eight percent, and the subsequent need to purchase a tail more than offsets any initial or subsequent savings from this type of insurance. Unfortunately, occurrence policies are not widely available today. Claims-made is favored by the insurance industry for this reason: If your policy is canceled or the company stops writing in your area, you are forced to buy an expensive tail, or else the company is off of the hook for any claims that arise after the policy lapses!

3. LIMITS: Policy limits are often expressed with two numbers, such as $100,000/$300,000 or $1,000,000/$3,000,000 and so on. The first number indicates the amount of

coverage for any one claim and the second number represents the total amount to be paid for all claims in that one-year period.   As an example, with a $100,000/$300,000 policy, the maximum amount to be paid out for any loss in that year will be $100,000 and the total amount to be paid for all losses in that year cannotl not exceed $300,000.   The $300,000 aggregate could be 100 cases of $3,000 each, or three cases of $100,000 each, but in any event, $300,000 is the maximum exposure for the insurance company for that year.   Presumably, awards in excess of policy limits will be uninsured and will come out of your pocket!   Often, a plaintiff's lawyer will sue for "punitive damages" which are not covered by malpractice insurance, or intentionally ask for more than the policy limits in order to scare the physician into settling, often for the maximum policy limits.

2 PHYSICIAN-PATIENT CONTRACT

A contract is a consensual agreement between competent adults as to mutually specified, or reasonably expected, duties or responsibilities.   Its origin was in the development of commercial transactions between merchants.   Each of the parties attempted to gain the maximum advantage from the bargain agreed upon.   When a patient utilizes the services of a physician, both enter into a contract for "services rendered".   This contract may be

   (1) Written,

   (2) Verbal, or

   (3) Implied.

An implied contract is just as enforceable as a written contract if it is appropriate.   Most often, this contract involves the patient actually choosing a physician based upon some referral source, such as his family doctor, a friend's recommendation, etc. The doctor and patient sit down and discuss the problem, information is exchanged, examination of the patient occurs, and the physician offers a diagnosis and course of treatment.   If the patient agrees with the treatment plan, then a contract occurs in which the physician agrees, for a certain fee, to try to the best of his or her ability, and utilizing the most up to date and accepted medical techniques or devices, to produce a result.   If that result is not obtained, a conflict arises which often finds its resolution in court.   It is important to examine some of the elements of that conflict.

For instance, treatment of a symptom such as pain may not result in an improvement, which may be measurable.   A cosmetic surgical result may be "reasonable" from the surgeon's point of view, but not what the patient expected, and so on. Secondly, the patient may claim that the result was not what he wanted or expected, or that the physician "promised" something else entirely. From the physician's side of the conflict, obstacles may have prevented the ideal result, such as noncompliance of the patient; a failure of some device beyond the control of the physician; a recognized and acceptable (medically) complication may develop; or, the results may be within the *acceptable norm*. In any event, without proper documentation, the dispute can become a shouting match. Curiously, even though most juries put enormous trust and credence in physicians, the plaintiff's case does not undergo as much scrutiny as the physician's because <u>the jury does not expect the plaintiff to be an expert.</u> The physician must prove his case! Again, this points out the need for good documentation. It is imperative that the physician documents the following in the course of his physician-patient contract:

1. That adequate information was given to the patient in the initial consultation for the patient to make a reasonable decision regarding treatment. This must also include mention of alternative methods of treatment, or the consequences of no treatment.

2. That the usual course of treatment was outlined along with expected outcomes and possible complications.

3. That the information was given to the patient by the physician and not relegated to a third party.

4. That the patient understood the information and alternatives prior to signing the consent form.

THE PRUDENT PATIENT TEST

In disputes regarding proper informed consent, the most important element is the *prudent patient test*. No liability can be ascribed to the physician if a "prudent person" in the patient's position would have accepted the treatment had he been adequately informed of all significant perils. Although this concept may be subject to reevaluation by hindsight, it becomes most meaningful where the treatment was lifesaving, urgent, or at least, prophylactic. It may be applicable to simple procedures such as the administration of antibiotics, where the dangers are commonly appreciated to be remote. In such cases, disclosure need not be extensive and the prudent patient test will usually prevail. Occasionally, however, simple procedures such as the administration of flu or pertussus vaccine become recognized as embodying serious medical risks of death or bodily harm. At that time, it becomes wise to include a full discussion of the risk and consent procedures in your practice even though the risks are remote. Some states apply the reasonable physician standard, which is what a reasonable physician would tell a patient under the same circumstances, but this is not as common as the prudent patient test.

3-CUSTOMER RELATIONS

The impression a patient gets about the doctor begins with the referral, whether it is from a friend, physician, or the yellow pages. It continues with the first phone contact with the office and then into the waiting room, with observation of the employees' demeanor, the length of time kept waiting, and finally with you -- the physician. At this point, your physical appearance, dress, demeanor, and willingness to listen become very important. Remember that the patient has made a very definite decision regarding how *good* you are long before you have even had a chance to speak! The atmosphere of the waiting room, the way the secretary smiles, the quality and age of the magazines available, general cleanliness, etc., all have a positive (or negative) effect on your "customer relations" regardless of how capable you might be. Some of the marketing skills currently being offered to us by commercial firms have been proven very successful in promoting both the practice and the image of physicians. Especially helpful are the practice brochures or newsletters, which can be sent to a patient upon his first phone contact with your office. This often develops a certain comfort level as it introduces him/her to you and your staff prior to the first visit. Legally or not, the doctor is truly the "captain of the ship". A bad attitude on the part of the receptionist, nurse, secretary, or other associates will be perceived as emanating from the physician as they are his extensions. Let any one of them be unfriendly or uncooperative and, surely, the doctor will be blamed! If a patient is late for an appointment, he should be dealt with kindly. But, if the doctor is late, he should apologize. Patients are, after all, as human as you and should be treated thus. They, too, have schedules to meet and places to go. The patient may have gone to a great deal of trouble just to make the appointment. A patient's privacy and dignity are also very important. The physician should always meet them when they are still fully clothed. A female attendant should be present during the examination of a female patient.

LISTENING The doctor must learn to listen to what his patient has to say. Many patients later complain, "The doctor didn't even listen to me". This may not necessarily be so, but there is a difference between "hearing" and "listening". In fact, the doctor may have spent a great deal of time listening to the patient. But if his attitude was pompous, or gave the impression that what the patient had to say wasn't important to him, then that patient will feel that the doctor didn't listen. The family should also be kept informed. Perhaps the member who accompanies the patient should be admitted into the consultation room if the patient so desires. Always keep the family aware of how things are progressing -- especially if the patient's condition is bad or worsening. Calling a patient on the phone to check upon his progress is a much-appreciated courtesy.

Patients remember very little of what is told to them, though it is very difficult for us to realize that[3]. This demonstrates the need for thorough documentation. All pertinent directions and warnings should be typed out on a letterhead or prescription blank and always retain a copy for your chart.

PRIVACY AND CONFIDENTIALITY.
A physician must never disclose what he has learned about a patient's private life or health in the course of his professional activities. that means that a medical report may not be sent to another physician unless he has the patient's written permission. this permission note should be kept in the patient's chart.

MAINTENENCE OF EXPERTISE

Doctors are required to "keep up" with the constantly expanding world of medical knowledge. This may be accomplished by reading appropriate medical journals and textbooks, by attending seminars, symposiums, or by participation in CME programs regularly.

CONSULTATION AND REFERRAL

A doctor is supposed to know the limits of his own ability and expertise. Sometimes more extensive testing can compensate this for this, but when those limits are reached, consultation or referral should be immediately considered.

ABANDONMENT

Failure to follow up on a patient -- even failure to notify him of a missed appointment and the need for further medical treatment, or the need to continue medications, etc. -- can lead to a charge of abandonment. Failure to see hospitalized patients regularly or frequently enough may also precipitate such a charge. Failure of the physician to document that he does not intend to take care of a given patient after a certain stated reasonable period of time, during which the patient should seek out another physician, may also result in a liability. It may be advisable, or necessary, to terminate the physician-patient relationship if the patient refuses to comply with medical advice. The physician should then send a letter of termination of care to the patient - via certified mail with a return receipt and a copy retained by the physician. In the letter, the physician should outline his reasons for discontinuing the relationship and should submit a list of suitable other doctors that the patient could see. Never list just one because that constitutes a referral, and you could be held liable for a referral! Remember that both common sense and good medical practice dictate that we take extra steps to provide competent continuity of care when discontinuing our services to a seriously ill patient!

4 INFORMED CONSENT

The term, "informed consent" usually applies to information given to patients about invasive procedures (diagnostic or therapeutic). "Shared decision making" is a term to describe the process whereby a course of treatment, such as the monitoring of a pregnancy and ultimate delivery, treatment of an illness, etc. is explained to a patient (and, perhaps, family) and a general understanding and agreement are reached. For the purposes of this discussion, however, we shall include both processes under "informed consent".

Both terms represent efforts to inform the patient, and often the family, regarding the medical problem and should bring various medical or surgical approaches into discussion. Consideration should be given to possible or probable complications and the likely outcome of such therapy. By such communication, the patient and family are better able to participate in or become apart of the medical care, both diagnostic and therapeutic-for better or worse! By taking the patient into the doctor's confidence and judgmental decision-making, the physician-patient relationship will be greatly strengthened and the likelihood of a malpractice suit, in the event of an unsatisfactory outcome is reduced. Conversely, the lack of informed consent or shared decision-making will result in a feeling that the patient might have opted out of the failed treatment had he been properly informed. Keep in mind that legal hindsight is far closer to 20/20 than medical foresight! The Minnesota case of Mohr vs. Williams[5] in 1905 is apparently the first of the modern cases dealing with informed consent. It involves an operation on the opposite (but worse) ear of a patient under general anesthesia. The consent was obtained for the other ear and the plaintiff (the patient) prevailed in court.

In 1914, Justice Benjamin Cardoso[6] later a U.S. Supreme Court Judge, ruled that the patient had an inalienable right "...to have done whatever he had agreed to (if medically and societally acceptable-- no one having the right to permit outright malpractice) upon his body, and also had a right to refuse anything else, even if it would be for his benefit." The modern requirement for informed consent was best stated in the case of Natanson vs. Kline[7]. It is now estimated that in lawsuits involving surgical care, a question of informed consent is raised in more than 10% of the cases and sometimes the decision as to the charge of a lack of informed consent will be the determining factor in the trial.

In the past, the mere writing by the physician in the hospital progress notes or in his regular office noted that the matter had been discussed with the patient and that the latter understood and had agreed to go ahead with the procedure was considered sufficient by most courts. New York[9] and Florida[8] have both ruled that the mere signing of an ordinary hospital consent sheet is not evidence of having obtained proper informed consent. These states now mandate the giving of written material, an audiovisual presentation, or at least a thorough face-to-face discussion by the doctor the patient. If this cannot be proved to the jury, their sympathy will usually be with the patient because they feel that, like themselves, the patient is NOT a medical expert and, therefore vulnerable to the suggestions of a doctor. This underscores the need for adequate documentation.

The Problem

In 1976, Doctors Robinson and Merav[3] tested patients for recall between four and six months following heart operations. They found that only 33% could remember the diagnosis and nature of their illness, 26% the proposed operation, 35% the risks of the procedure, 10% the potential complications, 29% the benefits, and 43% the alternative methods of treatment. The overall recall was an appalling 29%! Their conclusion: "This study calls attention to the fact that while patients were well-informed and comprehended their situations prior to operation, they subsequently forgot most of what they had understood and made other quantitative errors in their attempts to recall the consent interview. We believe it is essential to document, in some way, the details of informed consent so it becomes a permanent part of the clinical record, since memory of the event is unreliable." This could not be better stated. It is especially frustrating for a physician to have spent a great deal of time going over such details with a patient who later sues and in court accuses him of "not telling me anything!" Imagine how much more frustrating when the discussion was not documented!

DOCUMENTATION

Undoubtedly, the best method of documenting the informed consent discussion would be to use video or audiotaping of the event. This may prove cumbersome for the average physician, but some law firms to document their contractual arrangement with clients are presently utilizing both methods. As this method of documentation is a "real time" recording of the actual interview, it could also prove to be a double-edged sword if all of the necessary information was not actually discussed. Other problems associated with taping techniques involve storage and retrieval as well as the cost. Nevertheless, it has been proven effective by a New York medical malpractice company through the efforts of Charles P. Bailey, M.D., JD.

Other proven techniques for documentation of informed consent include the following:

1. Give the patient a written statement outlining the procedures, expected outcomes, and potential complications, on your office letterhead, with a "signoff" by the patient to acknowledge receipt. The patient's receipt, properly identified, becomes a permanent part of the patient's chart.

2. Use commercially available informed consent material with a similar signature for receipt.

3. Use audiovisual materials in the office, also with a signature receipt. And finally,

4. A personalized informed consent form (samples provided) with which the patient does more than simply sign a statement that he has been told of the risks and consequences.

Rather, he will write in long hand a statement to the effect that; "I have had a discussion with Doctor ____ regarding the proposed treatment, alternative(s), and the potential outcome. I understand these risks and possible complications and am willing to undergo the procedure." Being armed with proof that information had been given to the patient and the patient's own acknowledgment in long hand that such information was received and a decision reached would bring far greater weight in court than the mere statement by the physician that such information had been given.

WHAT CONSTITUTES INFORMED CONSENT? THE PATIENT MUST BE TOLD:

1) What his condition is in terms, which he will understand, including the probable outcome in terms of pain and suffering, disability, or shortening of life span.

2). What the doctor plans to do in terms of the likelihood of success, as well as the risks of complication, injury, or death. This need not be presented in statistical terms

3). What the risks of no therapy are, and finally

4). What therapy alternatives exist that might be offered by other physicians. The risk(s), and possible benefits, should be stated even if advising against such other approaches.

There are three categories of risks and complications that must be mentioned:

1). Those inherent in adjutant or supportive measures such as the risk of anesthesia, various drug therapies, or blood transfusions, etc.

2). Those risks inherent or specific to the particular contemplated procedure or program of treatment, such as bleeding, infection, or failure to achieve the desired result. Also, the likelihood of recurrence in malignancies, hernias, or sinus tract ablations. Very serious complications in some way related to the treatment such as blindness, paralysis, stroke, loss of limb and death must be specifically mentioned, despite their frequency, and "common complications" (greater than one percent) must also be mentioned.

3). All of the other infinitely numerous possible risks and complications may by summed up in some way such as: "Many things are still possible in the realm of medical treatment which cannot be anticipated but considered 'an act of God'. Unless you are willing to accept any and all of these possibilities, we may not be able to help you." The Judicial Council of the American Medical Association in 1984, in their "opinions" on practice matters, referred to informed consent in, stating:

> *"8.07 Informed consent: The patient's right of self-decision can be effectively exercised only if the patient possesses enough information to enable an intelligent choice. The patient should make his own*

determination on treatment. Informed consent is the basis social policy for which exceptions are permitted:

(1) Where the patient is unconscious or otherwise incapable of consenting and harm from failure to treat is imminent; or

(2) When disclosure poses such a serious psychological threat of detriment to the patient that it has to be medically contraindicated. Social policy does not accept the paternalistic view that the physician may remain silent because divulgence might prompt the patient to forego needed therapy. Rational, informed patients should not be expected to act uniformly, even under similar circumstances, in agreeing to or refusing treatment."

It must also be remembered that patients may refuse to listen or tell the doctor, "I don't want to hear any more", while the doctor is attempting to inform them of the risks. The patient must then be asked to express such refusal to be informed and their willingness to have the doctor do "whatever he thinks is best" in writing with their signature.

PATIENT RECALL

The impressive study by Doctors George Robinson and Avraham Merav in 1976 has been covered earlier in this chapter. In that study, patient's first efforts at recall resulted in a low of 10% to a high of 30% recall. Even after reviewing the tape recording there was still less than a 50% recall. Undoubtedly, anxiety and fear regarding the impending surgery accounted for much of that memory loss. Other phenomena such as paramnesia or distortion of memory may be involved, as well as confabulation in which the patient fills in the memory gaps by fabrications. It is therefore incumbent upon the physician to document the obtaining of informed consent to the greatest degree possible.

LEGAL FORMS OF CONSENT

There are three basic ways (legally) that consent to treatment may be obtained from a patient.

1) CONSTRUCTIVE: This is where the consent is understood without words from the nature of the situation such as in an emergency where the patient cannot express himself. No consent form is necessary in order to render true emergency care.

2) IMPLIED: The actions of the patient in response to a physician's suggestions constitute implied consent, such as a person pulling up his sleeve and sticking out his arm, essentially giving permission for the physician to give him an injection.

3) EXPRESS: Formalized consent, which is clearly stated, written or oral. It is an agreement to a proposed procedure based upon information given and received with comprehension and a subsequent statement of approval with or without limitations.

It is important to remember that consenting is two words: *informed* implying that information has been received and comprehended, and *consent* meaning that approval has been given. Except in true emergencies, courts will hold the physician responsible for the giving of the information upon which the decision to consent is made.

Can a surrogate, such as a nurse, paramedical person, pamphlet, or audiovisual program, give the information? The answer is yes, but the ULTIMATE responsibility still resides in the physician. While you may relegate SOME of that responsibility to another person, it would be extremely unwise to give the total responsibility to someone else. It should be remembered that the Avery giving of this information to a patient is a rapport-building process, which allows the patient to bond closer to the physician. In essence, it puts the patient "on the team" by allowing him to assist in the decision-making process.

SHARED DECISION MAKING[10]

In non-invasive types of therapy, information must still be given to the patient in order for him to make an intelligent decision regarding his care. Physicians are becoming targets of more lawsuits based upon "failure to warn", "failure to diagnose", or "failure to treat properly". It is therefore advisable that whenever a patient's ultimate prognosis is poor, or deterioration of the overall condition is expected, the physician should convey this information either to the patient, his family, or both. The appropriate treatments should be recommended. It may also be wise at this time to recommend a second opinion or referral of the patient to another treating physician of *higher authority*. It is essential in circumstances like these that the patient and/or the family be invited to take part in the decisions. That is why it is called *shared decision making* and, of course, it must be documented.

THE RIGHT OF SELF-DETERMINATION:

The patients' right of self-determination is protected by the courts. Under this umbrella, consent may be obtained expressly from the patient, or may be implied by the patient's conduct in an emergency. Permission from a parent or guardian is commonly required for minors or persons who are otherwise incapable of giving consent, except in emergencies and other special situations, such as abortions or giving of contraceptive devices. Failure to obtain consent to medical or especially surgical treatment creates possible liability under civil torts for assault (a threatening approach that puts someone in fear of a battery) and battery (an unlawful touching). **Lack of consent** cases are tried on concepts of "intentional torts", as opposed to negligence, and treat only the presence or absence of consent as a simple "yes" or "no" question and rarely addresses the quality of the care given.   This legal doctrine has evolved from a 1914 New York decision which declared that every human being of adult years and sound mind has the right to determine what should be done to his or her own body[6] and is known as the *Schloendorf decision*.   Careful documentation is essential and may be obtained through properly executed forms, entries in a patient's hospital chart or office record or other means.

However, the essential item is NOT the patient's signature, but rather the circumstantial PROOF that the patient made an INFORMED CHOICE before signing.   Documentation only provides some of that evidence.   It is the physician's duty to inform of those risks, which are most common and occur with some known frequency, or of those risks, which are very serious, despite the frequency.   Risks need not be disclosed if a physician does not know of it or should not have been aware of it in the exercise of ordinary care.   And, risk disclosure is not intended to unduly frighten a patient.   At least one court has stated "a physician would be guilty of bad medical practice if the patient were to be unduly alarmed by a complete detailed disclosure of all possible consequences of treatment beyond reasonableness". This would, therefore, put the physician at a disadvantage if the "laundry list" were TOO complete!

LEGAL STANDARDS FOR INFORMED CONSENT:

Three present methods are used in most states to determine legal standards of adequacy of informed consent.

1) The **Professional Standard**:   This is an older rule, which basically stated that the duty of a physician to disclose is limited to those procedures, which a prudent physician would make under similar circumstances.   This was based upon the Natanson vs. Kline decision.

2) The second approach, which is now used by a majority of states, rejects the conclusiveness of professional custom. Instead, it adopts the **"Reasonable Patient"** standard, which requires disclosure of information material to the patient's decision.   A risk is considered "material" when a reasonable person in what the physician knows or should know to be the patient's position would be likely to attach significance.   This is the risk, or cluster of risks, that the patient will weigh when deciding whether or not to forego the proposed therapy. This was based upon the Canterbury vs. Spence decision[11]

3) The third approach, established in a small minority of states, creates a statutory presumption that adequate disclosure has been made and informed consent has been obtained by means of a document containing specified information[12]. This approach is, however, the least common. Some states have ruled hospital consent forms to be legally worthless[8,9]. In most states now, because of the California case of Cobbs vs. Grant, a causal relationship between the injury received by the patient and the alleged act of malpractice must be established. This decision essentially states, "Had the revelation been given that the particular injury could have occurred, would a reasonable person have consented to the treatment?"

5-MEDICAL RECORDS

Medical records comprise all of the information pertaining to the care and treatment of a patient, including office visits, office consultation notes, hospital visits, operative reports, laboratory reports, and any and all records concerning the patient's care. The setting of the care is not important, that is, it may be office, hospital, some outpatient facility, home, or nursing facility. ALL records of the care of a patient through a particular episode or illness of that patient constitute the medical record for legal purposes. These records are medically important because they indicate the diagnostic efforts and conclusions, therapy given, and responses to that therapy. The medical record also documents the medical outcome from the disease state or injury, and is therefore of use to subsequent treating physicians in determining future care to the patient.

In this era of litigation, the medical record has become a double-edged sword! When the care rendered was appropriate and adequate, but the outcome adverse, it is this very record that will serve as the physician's lifeboat if a suit occurs. By the same token, the physician will "sink" in that lifeboat if the record is somehow lacking or incomplete!! The documentation provided in these records will ultimately prove conclusively to the jury that the physician acted in an appropriate manner. However, even in the case of good medical care, poor medical records can speak badly for or about the doctor and may help the plaintiff's attorney to convince the jury that the doctor was negligent. It is important to remember that malpractice litigation takes place long after the incident; therefore, the medical record is often the single most important item for the defense. "Perfect recall" on the part of the physician is extremely unconvincing to a jury, who are more likely to accept the perfect recall of the plaintiff- after all, they will reason, it did happen to the plaintiff, not the doctor! The burden of proof will be placed on the physician by the court, as the judge will instruct the jury, "if it has not been recorded, you may assume it was not done[14]."

LEGIBILITY

A record, which is legible, complete, accurate, and timely and permits the reconstruction of the patient's course of treatment, is a powerful defense weapon unless errors in care are evident. Conversely, a record which is sloppy, incomplete, or inaccurate, may not only be detrimental to the establishment of proper patient care (and in violation of JCAH standards), but may influence an attorney's decision to proceed with the claim. It may also destroy an otherwise good defense. The record must not only justify the diagnosis and treatment, but also resolve apparent conflicts by appropriate entries. This internal consistency, which is closely evaluated by attorneys, considers the interrelationship of the diagnosis, treatment, tests, X-ray and laboratory studies, medications, recommendations, and follow-up care, as well as consultants' reports, nurses' notes, and reports or notes by other health care workers. Any suggestion of blame, criticism, or discord, should be avoided since such conflicts will be exploited by a plaintiff's attorney[13].

ALTERING THE RECORD

Alterations, additions, or changes in the medical record may result in inferences of tampering, may also influence an attorney's decision to file a claim, or may result in the loss of an otherwise defensible suit. In some states, alteration of a medical record is grounds for criminal charges against the physician. Corrections in the chart should be done in a fashion, which will be discussed later in this section. Remember that the information contained in a medical record must anticipate its potential defensive needs in litigation. If you consciously think that a record COULD end up in court and make every entry in a clear, legible, concise, and complete fashion, the record will serve you well IF it ends up there. It has been recommended by some attorneys that progress notes be specific, yet sufficiently vague, to permit supplementation at deposition or trial. All events in the course of the patient's treatment should be recorded in the fashion of a chronicle without editorializing about the patient's attitude or compliance. However, failure to comply with medical advice, nurses' instructions, therapists, etc. should berecorded in a matter-of-fact fashion.

TELEPHONE CONVERSATIONS

Another area of documentation, which is important, is that of telephone communications. This is more often an office problem than one with the hospital, because the nurses' notes in the hospital chart always document the telephone conversations or attempted calls with doctors. These calls to or from patients MUST somehow be noted in the patient's record. Most offices use standard telephone message pads or some electronic medical record entry, which becomes part of the permanent record. Calls received or made while away from the office should be jotted down by the physician and later included in the patient's record. Medical advice given by telephone -- and not adhered to by the patient -- is just as likely to result in a suit, or at least, be PART of a suit as any other care. BE SURE TO DOCUMENT IT!

The majority of lawsuits derive from care given during hospitalization; therefore, one must concentrate heavily on the hospital medical chart. It is also this chart, which is the most often "violated", in that not only the attending physician makes notes here. It is common that house staff, consultants, associate physicians of a group practice, nurses, dietitians, physical therapists, social workers, QA nurses, and others write their observations in the chart. Therefore, it is imperative that during the course of medical treatment (not after) these notes be by the attending physician. If something is at variance with your observations or critical of your care, the entry should be discussed with the person who made it, and a correction entered by that person in properly prescribed manner. The WRONG thing to do is to start a "chart war" by WRITING how you disagree with the other observer. The plaintiff's attorney would just LOVE that!

Legally, these records belong to the hospital, clinic, nursing home, or individual doctor's office. The patient, however, has a right to the information accumulated and he has a legal right to obtain copies upon demand (even if his bill is unpaid!). Because of patient confidentiality laws, the doctor, hospital, or clinic,

may not furnish these records to any other doctor, lawyer, or third party, without the express written permission of the patient. However, these laws are waived in cases of Workman's Compensation and on requests from the patient's own insurance company in determination of benefit payments for services rendered.

The most serious deficiencies in the medical records are the following:

1. Copying, corrections or alterations;

2. Insufficiencies of recording;

3. Disappearance of the medical record; and

4. Alteration of a record and copying with the subsequent disappearance of the original will be deemed the equivalent of a forgery. The credibility of the physician or center will then be lost.

CORRECTION OF A MEDICAL RECORD

If some correction or addition MUST be made to a medical record, especially AFTER the commencement of a lawsuit, it should be done ONLY in the following manner:

1. Run a single line through the incorrect entry, preferably in different color ink

2. Make the new entry off to the side, after the original entry, or in some other OBVIOUSLY DIFFERENT area

3. Date (and time) the new entry and initial it.

The most important thing to remember is to NEVER erase or BLOT OUT the original entry. It must be legible, despite the correction. If you should be tempted to change a medical record after you are notified of a possible lawsuit, please THINK AGAIN. **By the time you have received such notification, the plaintiff's attorney has already received a copy of the original chart and reviewed it**[15,16]. Any alterations by you will automatically serve as an admission of guilt!

5-MALPRACTICE HAZZARDS IN THE OFFICE

One of the really important aspects of risk management is the issue of the doctor-patient relationship, which obviously begins at some finite point in time. For most physicians, that will be the first visit of the patient to the doctor's office. It may be a pleasant experience for both the patient and the doctor, or perhaps unpleasant for both. The interface between the patient and doctor in today's marketing parlance might be termed "customer relations". This subject comprises some of the common sense factors of the practice of medicine.

Though it may seem somewhat cliché', most people file lawsuits because of ANGER, usually arising from a PERCEIVED unexpected outcome of treatment. But, they usually don't sue someone that they like. And who is easier to like than their doctor? Yes, we have a definite advantage, which we don't often use. In fact, many times, without meaning to, we abuse the trust and admiration that patients naturally feel toward their physicians. How? Well, let's explore the problems.

THE MEDICAL ENVIRONMENT:

Though a patient's first encounter with a physician may be through the hospital emergency room, on consultation while a patient at the hospital, or in one of the hospital departments such as radiology, nuclear medicine, etc., most patients eventually meet with their doctor at his or her office. The office immediately takes on a personality that portrays something of the attributes of the doctor, perhaps in very subtle or obvious ways. The layout of the office waiting room, the decorating, diplomas, objects d'art and so on obviously say something about WHO you are or at least what your tastes are. This will undoubtedly strike some chord in the patient's mind. While I would not deign to dictate taste, it would behoove you to look at your office decorating with the mind of a stranger and see if it projects the image of you that you desire.

The waiting room should be designed for just that, "waiting". While every effort should be made to keep a patient's wait to a minimum, the room should be light, comfortable, and with some sort of entertainment media available: current magazines or newspapers, TV, music, or even patient education audiovisual devices. If your waiting room usually has a significant number of children include toys, games, or something to keep them occupied.

Remember that all of your patients have their own schedules to keep in their own complicated lives. Treat them as if they were all busy corporate executives. Keep their wait to a minimum, and when the scheduling is going to be delayed, keep them informed and allow them to either reschedule or leave the office for a while. It is very important that a FREE telephone be available for them as well as refreshments. The waiting room can also serve as a marketing tool while keeping the patient interested and entertained. The physical setup, however, is not only important in keeping the patient comfortable and entertained. It can also get you in trouble if the "walls are thin" between treatment areas or the receptionist or cashier, etc., private AND privileged conversations occur. If sensitive conversations can be overheard, at the least, it may make a potential patient somewhat defensive, embarrass or anger another, and at worst lead to charges of breach of confidentiality. Ensure that your office is adequately soundproofed.

KEEPING ON SCHEDULE:

While scheduling errors will always occur, try to minimize on overbooking and chronic lateness. A good "front office" staff will constantly communicate with the patients to inform them of approximate waiting time and alternate options. This will greatly reduce patient frustration and anger that could possibly push someone with a real problem over the edge into a lawyer's office. Your staff should be instructed NEVER to lie to the patient's and say, "The doctor will be with you shortly" when they know full well that you are one-half hour or more behind schedule. If the patient can be moved from the waiting room to a treatment room, this movement may be perceived as an encouraging sign that the Doctor is "on the way".

UNQUALIFIED MEDICAL ADVICE:

Your staff should be courteous and as solicitous as possible, but they should all be aware that the giving of medical opinion is only the responsibility of a nurse or physician, NOT the job of a secretary or receptionist. They should not offer medical advice or anecdotes because if bad advice or information is given by an unqualified employee and an injury results, the doctor could be held liable!

OFFICE POLICY:

In order to ensure consistency of performance, every organization has written "policy manuals". So should your office. This allows new persons to know just EXACTLY what is expected of them and thus, creates sort of a "legacy of behavior" in the office. Your employees should ALWAYS follow your policies and they should know that deviations from standard operating procedures only invite trouble. Deviations should be reviewed by you and your office manager and appropriate action taken. You should get into the habit of having periodic office meetings to discuss problems, staff gripes, etc. It is also a good idea to occasionally spot-check your charts for accuracy and completeness. You or a nurse, or even a junior associate could do this.

PERSONNEL:

The people who work for a physician are perceived by patients as EXTENSIONS of the physician both in attitude and deed, and their behavior, mannerisms, tone of voice, dress, etc., reflect those of their employer (at least as perceived by the patient). First impressions often last forever, but can only be made once. What a pity that a good, caring, and careful physician could make a bad impression on his/her new patient even BEFORE they meet! Lastly, remember that the attitude of your office personnel can affect your patients. Listen to your patients' as well as to your employees' complaints and act on them. An idea that is used in a good number of offices is a follow-up letter sent to patients *after* treatment, thanking them for being your patient and ASKING them to fill out a brief critique of how they felt they were handled. This serves several purposes. One, it lets you know how you are REALLY coming across to your patients and why. Second, it points out problem areas or people and, conversely, positive attributes and personnel. Last, it allows a patient to vent his/her ire and anger and gives you a chance to do something about it BEFORE they get to a lawyer! It's an inexpensive but very useful communications tool.

6-THE ANATOMY OF A MALPRACTICE SUIT

Perhaps the best way that I can introduce this topic is to recommend a book that you will enjoy reading.   One of our colleagues, Howard C. Snider, Jr., M.D. from Alabama wrote about his experience with a malpractice trial, in a book called "Jury of My Peers".   The book is easily readable as it written almost in a fictional style, but it makes the experience of being sued very personal.   He very adequately describes the mechanism of the legal process and the subsequent emotional travails that are experienced by the defendant.   I would recommend that you read this book (before you are sued).   Having introduced the topic, I shall now take you through a lawsuit as it develops, in order to afford you an understanding of the entire process.   As you will see, there are numerous legalistic steps along the way which must be followed by BOTH the defense AND the plaintiff's lawyers. These steps have been formalized both by tradition and statutes and may vary a little from state to state, but the general process remains the same.

THE INCIDENT:

An incident is any thing which has occurred about which you suspect there might be a problem pending.   This is the untoward event, the "therapeutic misadventure", the "surgical disaster", or whatever, that causes the patient to seek legal redress.   In some cases a simple and sincere apology by the physician to the patient would help to defuse the situation. A patient who left in a disgruntled frame of mind might have had an attorney request his records; the patient may have quarreled over his bill; there may have been an accident in the office; or, an angry patient may have said "I'll sue".   Many things can signal an incident.   When this occurs, what should the physician do?

1. Communicate with the patient.   This is your best chance to avert a legal situation from developing.   Try to find out why the patient is unhappy or angry, and see if there is anything (within reason) that could be done to improve the situation (if possible).   Once the patient has contacted a lawyer, however, this avenue is closed as communication with the patient is prohibited. If the patient has an outstanding balance on the medical bill, and they are very upset over a complication or bad outcome of treatment, it might be wise to "write off" the bill -- and let the patient know that you are doing so out of good will.   If the patient believes that you are sensitive to their

situation, they may be less likely to consult an attorney. However, I would not advise compromising your principles ONLY to avoid a lawsuit.

2. Notify your insurance company. Your insurer, or his agent, must be notified of the incident. Use a registered letter, return-receipt requested, even if a phone call has been made. You want proof of this being done. It must be done as soon as you are aware of the potential suit. Your insurer will look into the situation and probably request certain things from you. Cooperate in every way, for the insurer is protecting your interest(s). It is critical that an incident be reported as soon as it arises because that is the best time for investigators to gather information. Two years from now a nurse may have quit or moved across the country. The attending physician may have retired or you may be in a different state. There is no time like the present to report an incident. It is also by receipt of the incident report that the insurance company can set aside money for a potential claim.

3. Write your recalled impressions. You should immediately write everything down you can remember about the patient which would have a bearing on the situation, including the names of personnel involved, and the comments made while it is fresh in your mind. The original chart must not be touched – no Alterations, addenda, corrections, or other changes are permissible. The chart, for all purposes, was "sealed" when you finished it. Write what you will on all the paper you desire, but do not place one dot on the chart!

4. Keep quiet. Do not discuss the case with your friends or colleagues, except possibly those involved in the case. Under no circumstances discuss it with any attorney, except, if you wish, your own. When discussing it with colleagues who may be involved, discuss facts only and venture no opinions or conjecture. Remember, they, too, may become involved in any subsequent suit and essentially may be in a position to harm you while protecting themselves. Keep your opinions to yourself and offer no comments.

5. If the patient or family asks questions, they must be handled politely and diplomatically, but only the requested verifiable information may be given and only with proper releases. Frequently, we are asked, "Will reporting incidents jeopardize one's insurability or raise rates?" The answer is "no". For early and accurate incident reporting is valuable to the insurer and he will look more kindly toward the insured that cooperates. Also, incidents on file which later become suits will serve as a "tail" for that particular incident, even if the insurance policy has lapsed or been dropped.

THE LETTER OF INTENT:

While it is absolutely true that anyone in the United States may sue anyone else for ANYTHING, it is also true that a malpractice suit is VERY EXPENSIVE for an attorney to litigate. Therefore, if an attorney with an established reputation in medical malpractice decides to take a case, he intends to WIN IT! It may bring you some comfort to know that the majority of attorneys will not take a questionable case and even a good case has only about a one-in-ten chance of bringing a verdict FOR the plaintiff. However, this will be little comfort once you have been notified of the initiation of a suit. Don't even think of finding some nefarious way of convincing the attorney that he can't win, because at this point the "die is cast".

Once the attorney has done some preliminary investigation and decides that this case is worth pursuing, his office will issue a legal document known as a "letter of intent". This will be a very matter-of fact letter, usually written to you on the letterhead of his firm, stating that legal action is being pursued. At this point, after your nerves have settled, you are advised to take certain immediate steps:

    1. Contact your malpractice carrier. It is not uncommon that the filing of a suit is the physician's first inkling of trouble. Whether you had previously reported the case as an "incident", or the suit was a complete surprise, you must now notify your insurer immediately.

    2. Take all legal papers received after copying them for your own files, and send them to your insurer or his agent, certified mail, with return-receipt requested. In most states, there is a specified period of time, (usually 20 days), during which the papers must be answered. Waste no time in getting them to the insurer.

    3. Write down your recollections of the case, including the names of all other involved personnel, etc. It will never be fresher in your memory than now.

    4. Obtain your office records on the patient as well as the hospital records for the period in question. You should review all these documents at this point and dictate a "case summary" which will be sent to your malpractice carrier and the defense lawyer, which they (or you) will select. The case summary should contain all of the medically important facts of the case in a chronological fashion, without editorializing. It would be a very wise thing at this time to make four COMPLETE COPIES of your records and put the original into a large SEALED manila envelope and deposit it within a safe. Why? Well, first, this will remind you that NO CHANGES are to be made in the record and also to keep the original intact and safe for trial. The copies will be sent to the insurance company, the defense and plaintiff's attorneys, and there will be one for you to review.

5. It is even more important now that you discuss this with no one except the immediate staff who needs to help you prepare the case, your defense attorney, and the insurance company representative. If you discuss the case with your colleagues, you may find yourself in the embarrassing position of finding out that one of them has agreed to be an expert for the plaintiff!

THE DEFENSE ATTORNEY:

Your insurer will appoint an attorney to handle your defense and he will want to arrange an interview with you to discuss the case, get the facts, and get to know you. He is your defender, your guardian angel. You will get to know each other very well in the coming months. Be frank, straight forward, and honest with him. He is not judging you, but rather, is going to attempt to prove you are not guilty of negligence, or of violating the standards of sound medical practice. It would be much easier for him to do this if he learns to like you and respect you. Treat him accordingly. Although your insurer is paying his fee, legally speaking, this attorney is representing you in the suit. Learn all you can about him and help him in every way possible. If, however, there is a marked personality conflict, or if you have a good reason to believe he is not up to the task, contact your insurer about the possibility of changing attorneys. Your insurer, however, usually knows more about the local defense attorneys than you do, since insurance companies have cause to deal with them more often; they usually know the best in the area. After all, it's their money on the line!

YOUR OWN ATTORNEY:

Do you need your own lawyer? Well, a lot has been said about hiring your own because of the fact that the attorney chosen by the insurance company basically represents the best interests of the company. That is true, but usually, that coincides with your best interests. Your own attorney will certainly increase legal costs (to you) and may "get in the way" if he or she is not competent in the field of medical malpractice. If the money damages being sought by the plaintiff exceed your policy limits, then it could be advisable to hire your own attorney to protect your interests. Your insurer will send you a letter in that case advising you, at your own discretion, to call in your own defense. The purpose of this additional lawyer is NOT to assist the malpractice defense attorney, but rather to protect you regarding the amount above the insurance company's limit, should the judgment in the case exceed that limit. Only you, after adequate consultation, can make the decision as to whether or not it is worth the added expense for the additional protection afforded.

A WORD ABOUT ANGER:

One of the most important elements in medical malpractice litigation is the physician-defendant's feelings. How those feelings are expressed and controlled may have enormous influence on the outcome of the suit. Predictably, physicians react differently than, say, businessmen when informed of a suit against them, possibly because we tend to have the temperament of artists. A lawsuit alleging medical malpractice means (to US) that our WORTH as a physician is being questioned and that goes right to the core of our being. After all, we sincerely try to put our entire effort, knowledge, and ability into EVERY case, not just selected cases. How could ANYONE accuse us of doing SUBSTANDARD work? We must recall, that like it or not, our legal system is ADVERSARIAL and it is the job of the opposing attorney to portray his "adversary" (YOU) in the worst possible light. The plaintiff's attorney will try to create his own version of reality in which the doctor-defendant will appear like Doctor Frankenstein. It will not serve his case well to be honest and say that you are a good and careful physician whose patient had an unfortunate outcome of good medical care. The anger that is generated in the average physician often promotes behavior that is counter-productive. Some physicians will react by calling the plaintiff's lawyer and ventilating their feelings. The plaintiff's lawyer will gladly act as a psychologist, listen to everything you say, and then later use it against you in court! Sometimes the anger just smolders and later erupts during a deposition or in court, making the physician look bad and giving the opposing attorney more reason to make your life miserable. Remember, other than money, hostility towards the defendant is one of the major motivational factors for plaintiff's attorneys. And what about the defense attorney, YOUR attorney? Other than his hourly wage, your behavior and attitude are among the very few things that will motivate him or her to work hard for you. If your lawyer is convinced of your truthfulness and honesty and is convinced that you and your family are being wrongfully hurt by what's happening to you, then he's going to work extra hard in your behalf. If your case actually goes all the way to trial, here's something you might expect from the plaintiff's lawyer: He will try to confuse your feelings towards him. If he was gentlemanly and courteous at your deposition, he might come at you like a Sherman Tank at trial and try to tear you to pieces. Or, if he was aggressive and rude at the deposition, he might put on his best manners in court and allow you to try to react defensively or aggressively so as to impress the jury with what an evil person you really are. Another thing that we physicians have to realize and accept as the suit goes on is that the defense lawyer knows what he's doing.

You should work with him, be honest and instructive so that the two of you work as a team. Above all, strive to impress the jury of your decency, truthfulness, and your ability to control your feelings. What about the effect of the lawsuit on you? Don't think that you will be unaffected. Most of us will undergo personality changes, which will be noticed by your staff, other patients, and most importantly, your family. Make every effort to communicate and ventilate your feelings so that those most close to you can help you and not feel shutout. You may even seek out a physician support group to attend when the pressure becomes too great. You may have been trained to think that you are superhuman, but beneath the white lab coat or green scrub suit, we are all as human as the next guy!

INTERROGATORIES:

After an attorney has agreed to take on a malpractice case for a plaintiff, they must, by law, accumulate facts. The first of these facts are an opinion, by a qualified expert, that you MAY, indeed, be guilty of malpractice. This usually occurs in a specified period of time following the "letter of intent". Next, they will query you on some very basic facts relating to your professional qualifications as well as some facts "as you see them" about the case in question, but usually, these are very general in nature. These questions will arrive in the form of a questionnaire called an "interrogatory", and your attorney will also send one to the plaintiff. The best advice regarding the offer information not specifically asked for. Usually, your attorney will work with you in answering the interrogatory. Always ask him. The completed interrogatory should be sent to your attorney NOT the plaintiff's even if they give you a stamped, self-addressed envelope. The period of time from the Letter of Intent until you receive the interrogatory may vary from one to six months.

DEPOSITIONS:

The examination before trial, or deposition, is a part of the discovery process, a method by which each side attempts to find out as much as possible about the other side's position, thinking, information, and weaknesses. These are fact-finding sessions that both sides will stage and they are semi-formal, often in either lawyer's office or possibly in the office of a court-reporting firm. While the setting may be informal, the content of the recorded deposition is VERY FORMAL and can (and will) ultimately be read to the jury to cast doubt on your testimony should you say something in court that is at variance with your deposition!

1) Prepare yourself for the deposition and rehearse with your attorney. This includes assembling all material(s) requested and being generally

ready. Do your homework and the study the medical aspects of the case, as this is where you are an expert (in comparison with any lawyer).

2) Answer carefully and honestly. The atmosphere in most depositions is far less formal than in a courtroom. However, the deposition is taken under oath and will be recorded verbatim. The answers given are, of course, admissible in court. If you do not understand the question, do not answer until it is made clear, even if this should require multiple attempts. This question, and its answer, is to be recorded. Wherever possible, the best answer is a simple "Yes", "No", or "I don't know".

3) Do not volunteer any information. Make the plaintiff's attorney do his job. He has to search for the information he wants, so don't make it easy for him. Remember, it is NOT your job to give the plaintiff's attorney an education in medicine. Any knowledge that he may learn about the medical facts of the case he should get on his own with as little help from you as possible! Answer a question accurately and completely, but stop there. DO NOT EMBELLISH! You are not, under these circumstances, talking to a judge and jury, trying to explain your actions, and why you did what you did. Therefore, give only what is requested and never attempt to "educate" the plaintiff's attorney. Many doctors, not knowing the legal game, mistakenly believe that by being smarter than the other lawyer and presenting all the facts, he will realize that he "got it all wrong" and cancel the lawsuit. In fact, he may even try to lead you to believe that by the tone of some of his questions. But, DON'T BE FOOLED. Any information that he obtains at this session can, and will, be used against you, and you will NEVER talk him out of suing you--not by being nice, not by being nasty, not by anything you do or say. However, he will be sizing you up as to the kind of a witness you will make in court, so that he will be able to rattle you and bring out your worst behavior in court for the jury's benefit. Don't guess at answers. It is perfectly proper to state, "I don't know," or "I don't remember," when this is the case. Such a statement is far better than guessing. If your guess is wrong, it is embarrassing, not to mention deleterious to your case, when the jury is told that your answer was wrong.

4) Use your chart. Whenever possible, refer to the materials at hand when answering, rather than trusting your memory. If your memory is incorrect, your answer will easily be proven incorrect. It will, likewise, reflect poorly on subsequent answers from memory. This is another example of why a well-kept chart is so important.

5) Be polite to the opposing attorney, and attempt to appear concerned and even contrite. Try not to anger or outsmart the opposing attorney --your behavior WILL come back to haunt you at trial!

6) Follow your attorney's lead. If your attorney objects to a question, do not answer it until he instructs you to do so. He is your guide and must be used as such. He is there to defend you, and although you may know the answer, do not give it unless he instructs you to do so. Further, bring nothing into a deposition without checking with him and let him solve any conflicts you may have over the wording of a question.

7) *Authoritative sources*: For the purposes of a deposition or at trial, you are NEVER to agree with the plaintiff's attorney that ANY textbook, article, or monograph, etc., related to your case is AUTHORITATIVE. If you do, then ANYTHING in that source is automatically agreed to by you. The attorney will find some sentence in the book at variance with your case and will remind the jury that you agree that the source in question is authoritative and thus, will "blow you out of the water!!" The proper reply to the question, "doctor, do you feel that this book, article, etc., is authoritative?" is the following: "No, the field of medicine is too vast for any one source to be totally accurate and authoritative in all aspects. I do, however, believe the information that you just quoted from the source is in agreement with my management of the case." This reply will not please the plaintiff's attorney!!

HOW TO ASSIST YOUR ATTORNEY:

It has been said by many defense attorneys that most malpractice cases, regardless of the effort put in by them, are won or lost by the physician. Why? There are many reasons. Perhaps the most important is the fact that juries WANT to acquit a doctor and WANT to believe his or her explanation of the medical facts of the case. If the demeanor of the doctor is somewhat less than professional, or what they might expect to be unprofessional behavior, then they might subconsciously prejudge the doctor as "substandard". Another reason is that, despite all of the preparation for trial and previous experience that a lawyer may have, the truth is that the physician still knows infinitely more about medicine and in greater depth than the attorney. This is true for both the defense and plaintiff's attorneys, but, presumably, it would be to the physician's benefit to be certain to share his knowledge only with the defense attorney. This can be accomplished first by giving as little information as possible to the plaintiff's attorney at deposition as previously discussed, but more importantly, by assisting your attorney as much as possible in the pretrial discovery, in the deposition of witnesses, preparation of graphic aids for trial (for the benefit of the jury), and most importantly, by working as a TEAM. You should listen very carefully to all of your lawyer's advice regarding style of dress, methods of controlling facial expression, proper demeanor, etc. Maybe the most important words that I will write in this entire course are the following: DO NOT EXPECT A TRIAL TO BE A SEARCH FOR THE TRUTH. IT IS PURELY AND SIMPLY A BATTLE BY BOTH SIDES TO WIN BY ANY MEANS POSSIBLE. A TRIAL IS MORE CLOSELY AKIN TO THEATRE THAN A SCIENTIFIC SEARCH FOR THE TRUTH. THE BEST PLAYERS REAP THE REWARDS! As cynical as that may seem, it happens to be the truth. Rather than run from it, you will be best served to learn to USE it to your advantage. Dress the part and act the part of the learned and kindly physician who CARES. Carefully follow the prompts that your attorney will provide.

HOW TO ASSESS THE ABILITY OF YOUR ATTORNEY:

We have previously mentioned the fact that, for the most part, it is unnecessary to hire your own attorney. But, what if you feel that the insurance company's lawyer is not up to the task? You may have "bad vibes" with this attorney, or you might have good reason to believe he or she is incompetent. If such were the case, it would be a good idea to be up-front with the attorney regarding your feelings. After a face-to-face chat, you may resolve your differences or the attorney may decide to turn your case over to someone else in the firm. These feelings should also be communicated to the insurance company because they have a vested interest in the outcome of the case. Any feelings of mistrust or enmity MUST be resolved EARLY in the process, however, so that if a new attorney is chosen he or she has adequate time to prepare.

THE EXPERT WITNESS:

Most states require that prior to actually filing a lawsuit that a plaintiff's attorney has IN HAND an opinion of a recognized expert in the appropriate field, that the care involved in the case fell below the proper standard. The doctor who renders that opinion may or may not be the actual expert who agrees to testify against you, but it IS on the basis of that opinion that the plaintiff's attorney decides to file suit. In the ensuing months an expert witness will be found, and, depending on the complexity of the case, several experts may be used. Many states have recently enacted legislation to require expert witnesses to be just that, expert. They must have been active in practice in the specific field in question in the past 5 years in order to qualify as an expert -- but not in all states. You had best check with your attorney regarding the law in your state, but IF the adverse witness IS an unqualified "whore", your attorney should be able to use that information to good advantage. This information usually comes out at the expert's deposition, which occurs close to trial. So, what about the "good guy"? It is usually YOUR responsibility to find an expert IN your field and usually, IN your community (loosely speaking, the "community" can be in the general region of your practice within the state). When you chose an expert, you must remember the rules of the THEATRE. He or she must LOOK credible, SOUND credible, and ACT credible as well as being a recognized expert. Sadly, it serves your cause better to choose a fairly well credentialed physician who looks and talks like Marcus Welby than to obtain a world-renowned professor who looks and acts like Edward G. Robinson or Jack Palance, or the staff of "Saint Elsewhere"! It will definitely reflect badly on your chances of winning if the jury dislikes or disbelieves your expert(s).

SETTLEMENT OFFERS:

After the rigors of discovery are over, and all depositions completed, your insurer will assess the "worth" of the case, that is, what dollar amount a jury verdict might bring. This will be compared to the strength/weakness ratio of the defense's case to the plaintiff's case, the damage as evaluated, the locale, the judge, and previous results in similar cases, to obtain a perception of the chances of winning the case for you as well as the cost of carrying it through trial. These statistics will be carefully evaluated by a committee of accountants, lawyers, and actuaries and a realistic settlement offer may be reached. Settlement is not an admission of negligence or liability, but rather, an agreement by the plaintiff to discontinue the suit in return for a predetermined sum of money. This is often perceived by the physician as "blackmail", and in a way it is. It amounts to a realistic assessment by the insurance company that they are willing to spend that sum of money (the settlement offer) rather than spend more just to get the case heard in court even if the chances of winning are good. However, there is a break-even point, and beyond this point, it probably is worth "going for broke". Most physicians have the right of approval of settlement in their policies, so you must approve the offer. If you approve, it is suggested that the agreement specify that neither party may disclose the terms of agreement to the media. In addition, the document must state that it is not an admission of liability. In any event, whether you end up paying a settlement, or lose at trial, the amount paid out will be reported to the Department of Professional Regulations, and ultimately to a newly- formed computer bank of such information being compiled by the government (Big Brother?). It is often to the physician's advantage to settle promptly because of the cost of being away from the practice and the coronary wear-and-tear. It is obviously also to the insurer's advantage as costs escalate daily in a suit (win or lose). It is often difficult to convince a physician to settle, however, because of professional pride. But it usually makes good sense.

THE TRIAL

Even if the trial takes two weeks, it is almost an anticlimax after all of the emotional gut wrenching that you have been through by the time you get to trial. It will, however, make a lasting impression on you! By the time it is over, unless you are an emotionally bereft zombie, you will accept ANY verdict, just to have it over with. You will have become emotionally labile and difficult to live with. Probably, you will have lost several nights of sleep. However, two thoughts should be of some comfort: Doctors win the majority of malpractice suits, and IF you lose, you won't go to jail or be executed. (Also, if you lose, usually only the insurance company will pay any money). With that in mind, let's look at what you will encounter.

PRETRIAL PREPARATION:

Usually, beginning about six weeks prior to trial, you will be asked by your attorney to review all of the depositions of the witnesses and the medical records pertinent to the case. Some of this work will be done by you at your office and at home, but eventually, you will begin to make visits with the attorney to discuss what you know and feel and in general, to plan strategy. You should be using as much time as you can to MEMORIZE the medical chart related to the patient's care, and to read as much as you can regarding the medical facts of the case so that you don't stumble over any facts at trial. You should also use this time to get to know your attorney, and hopefully, for him to know you. You might take him or her out to dinner before or after some of the preparation sessions, and include your spouse in on these personal sessions, both for prevention of marital discord and also so your attorney can see you and your family (if you have one) and appreciate the totality of your suffering. He'll work harder for you if he likes you and sees how this lawsuit is hurting you and those around you.

VISUAL AIDS

You and only you are best prepared to help your attorney present a cogent defense. You know the medical facts, you know what you did, or didn't do, and you know how to present medical facts to laymen (your patients). Try to be creative, and devise or purchase some visual aids that will help the jury UNDERSTAND the key points of the case. NOT just pictures will suffice. After all, you can bet that the plaintiff's attorney will have some photos, or a video of "a day in the life of..." etc. This is THEATRE, BIG DRAMA. You must out-do the other side by MAKING SURE THE JURY UNDERSTANDS WHAT YOU AND YOUR EXPERTS ARE SAYING!!! Pick out key issues and create or have created for you some kind of mannequin, or three-dimensional object that adequately displays what you are trying to explain. In the book, "Jury of My Peers", Dr. Snider, in attempting to explain how difficult it is to dissect out the ureter in a pelvis filled with adhesions from previous cancer surgery and subsequent irradiation, used a glass bowl filled with some fruit and grapes as the intestines and two long pieces of spaghetti as the ureters all glued together with "Superglue". This aided immeasurably in the ability of the jurors to understand the difficulty in REAL terms. You can use your own ingenuity to adapt this type of display to your own specific needs. Believe me, it's worth the extra effort. And besides, a little "play therapy" could provide some needed relief from the tedium of the pretrial period.

HOW TO DRESS FOR TRIAL

There may be some regional differences, and the ultimate authority on this is your attorney, but in general, you should look PROFESSIONAL, UNOSTENTATIOUS, AND DIGNIFIED. Dress as if you were a department head of a big corporation. For men, a blue suit with pin stripes and a "regimental" red and blue-striped tie is an acceptable outfit. Jewelry such as tie-tacs, cufflinks, gold bracelets, or fancy wedding bands are OUT. The watch should be an inexpensive Timex or digital with a black band. A Rolex or Piaget, etc is definitely OUT! Women usually have better imagination on how to dress low-key (what to wear to the husband's boss' reception?) so I'll leave that for you to decide if you are a woman. The same rules of conservatism apply. Again, consult your attorney for the fine points. You're probably thinking, "This is stupid! What does it have to do with a trial?" Well, in rational terms, nothing, but in the context of dealing with the American Legal System, EVERYTHING!! So, take it very seriously!

THE BEGINNING OF THE TRIAL

By now, your emotions have been pumped up to the point of emotional fatigue, but you will find yourself ready for action, not unlike getting ready for the "big game" when you were in college. The courtroom setting is usually somewhat dreary, filled with all kinds of characters that look seedy and more or less like they belong on a "Cops & Robbers" TV show. You will, no doubt, feel out of your element and very much intimidated. Once you enter the courtroom, you will notice the Judge's bench in the front of the room and some space set aside for witnesses and the court reporter. There will also be a court official, the Bailiff, whose job it is to maintain the order of the court, and attend to the jury.   On one side of the room is the seating for the Jury, and then the seating for the spectators, divided between those on the defendant's side and those on the plaintiff's side.   There may be a long table or two for the plaintiff and his lawyers and the defendant and his lawyers. One of the first official tasks that the judge and the lawyers will undertake is the selection of the jurors.   This process is known as the Voir dire.

THE VOIR DIRE:

Attorneys take this process very seriously and many books have been written on the psychology of jury selection.   It is a bit of a chess game whereby through a series of questions and answers, the lawyers on each side attempt to DE-select various potential jurors.   Each potential juror removed is called a STRIKE and each lawyer can use only around three strikes, to whittle down a panel of from 20 to 100 potential jurors to a final six or twelve and one alternate.   As previously mentioned, each potential juror is asked questions by both lawyers, usually about their background and feelings about various things that relate the issues in the trial.   This is done in order to get a feel for which way that potential juror might vote -- for the plaintiff or the defendant.   Each lawyer, in turn, will "strike" potential jurors that they feel may be adverse to their cause.   These are "preemptory strikes" and are limited in number, depending upon the size of the panel of potential jurors assembled by the judge. However, strikes "for cause" are unlimited in number and have to do with a predisposition of the potential juror such as being a relative of one of the parties in the suit, or extreme prejudice by virtue of profession or life experiences.   In some cases, a professional psychologist, trained in the techniques of the Voir Dire is used to help in this selection.   You can also be a great help to your attorney by communicating your "gut reactions" to him/her during this process.   It is not a comforting thought that, no matter HOW well prepared you are and HOW GOOD your case may be, ultimately, your chances may depend upon WHO is sitting on the jury!! The process usually takes the morning of the first day of trial, and typically, the judge calls a recess for lunch after which the trial begins.

The ritual of the trial starts with the opening statements given by each side.   The Plaintiff's lawyer gets to go first and end last at the close of the trial.   The opening statements are emotional appeals by each side to set the stage for the jury in the hopes of gaining their sympathy.   Nothing said by the lawyers at this point is evidence, only feelings, and the judge reminds the jury of this.   Nevertheless, a powerful opening statement and closing argument can have a definite effect upon the outcome. This is usually the point in the trial where the oratorical prowess of the respective lawyers is displayed.

THE WITNESSES:

The entire conduct of the trial is by rote, that is, it follows a carefully prescribed outline. The plaintiff will present its side first and that means that the jury will hear the plaintiff's side of the "story" along with all supporting witnesses, expert, or otherwise. Of course, during the process of obtaining testimony supporting their case, the defense attorney will cross- examine each of the plaintiff's witnesses and probe for weaknesses in their testimony and attempt to discredit them in the process. If their testimony in court differs in some way from their sworn deposition, the appropriate parts of the deposition will be read aloud to the witness and the jury to show confusion of the witness or, perhaps embellishment. This will usually create an impression that the witness is unreliable. Remember this well when it is your turn to be a witness! You have two chances, the first occurs when you are the plaintiff's ADVERSE witness, perhaps, a witness against yourself. Later, you will be examined DIRECTLY by your attorney when you will be asked to give explanations in your defense. The thing to remember all during the trial is that you must KEEP YOUR COOL!! When you hear testimony that you disagree with, don't show ANY emotion. Don't shake your head, or screw up your lips as the plaintiff's expert espouses some obvious (to you) medical nonsense or outright lies. Don't be surprised --that's what the plaintiff's lawyer is paying them to do. Or, perhaps the learned gentleman (or woman) truly believes he or she is serving a noble purpose by telling the jury how medicine "should have been practiced", and how, if only you had done what he "always" does, the result would have been different. No matter. This is what the adverse expert is being paid to do whether or not he truly believes in his testimony. The main thing is to remember that you must show no emotion and listen very carefully and take notes. Before your lawyer cross-examines him, he will confer with you to learn what weakness to probe. Keep cool so that you can assist your attorney!

YOUR TURN AS WITNESS:

As we have discussed, you have two turns as a witness. One time you will be DIRECTLY examined by the plaintiff's attorney and CROSS-EXAMINED by your attorney. Later, the opposite will occur. Though you will have an easier time when you are being DIRECTLY examined by the Defense, the rules of conduct are the same. While under Direct examination, it is not permissible for the attorney to "lead the witness", that is to use expressions such as, "isn't is true that..?", but an attorney on Cross-Examination can lead you.   This is the rule, but invariably both sides will break it and the opposite attorney will object loudly and the judge will rule. Remember ALWAYS to follow your attorney's lead. DON'T answer a question to which an objection has been raised until YOUR attorney gives you the OK.   While you are an adverse witness (against yourself) try to keep your answers as short as possible and ALWAYS give the same answers as you did at your deposition, as we have previously covered.   If you HONESTLY have changed your mind about an answer, be prepared to CALMLY give an explanation as to WHY you are changing your answer (only if asked, of course). A proper response to the question, "But doctor, on ...date, didn't you say....?" is, "Well, yes, I did, but since that time I have put a great deal of study into this matter, and upon further reflection I believe that my answer at deposition was in error." Of course, you must be prepared for a rebuttal to the effect of, "Oh, so your memory of the event is even CLEARER now that more time has passed since your deposition, eh?"   Remain calm and say, "No, I didn't say that.   I simply feel that after studying the case so much that my first answer was, perhaps a bit reflexive, but not really representative of what occurred." And so on.   Keep remembering at all times that your ONLY defense is honesty and integrity.   You MUST impart that image to the jury. If the plaintiff's lawyer begins to try to "tear you up", to try to make you angry, you must "rise above it" and answer politely and courteously, perhaps with a slightly hurt look on your face. Believe me, he will TRY to portray you as TOTALLY inept, mean, uncaring, curt, rude, arrogant, etc.   You CAN counter this ploy with a little acting yourself.   But you can't lose your temper or patience.   One emotional outburst by you and he's won the game. But IF you keep your cool, you will make him seem foolish and overbearing and win the sympathy of the jury.   Prior to this point in the pretrial preparation, your lawyer will have coached you in the fine-points of "legal drama".   If you heed his coaching well and don't get "rattled", you will do just fine.   When it is finally your turn to speak in your behalf, you will feel a great relief!   After all, for several days (or even weeks) now, you've been subjected to humiliation and mud-slinging and outright lies and now it's your turn to "set the record straight". This is truly your moment -- so take full advantage of it.   The strategy of your testimony will have been practiced with your attorney for weeks right up to this morning.   You should have prepared or had prepared for you various visual aids that you can demonstrate to the jury.   You will now have their FULL ATTENTION. Talk TO them as if you were a learned professor, but NEVER talk over their heads.   Deliberately make eye contact with each and every juror to make sure that they understand what you are saying.   Remember that they REALLY WANT TO BELIEVE YOU so don't screw up your best chance!   Using your props take them through every facet of the important points of your defense.   Show them how the "adverse event" occurred, the difficulties you encountered, the problems the patient had and so on.   Be sincere and convincing. ALWAYS show concern for the anguish of your patient and sympathy for his or her suffering. Don't appear cold and uncaring. Your job is to convince them that you did your very best in caring for your patient and that the adverse event was NOT due to malpractice. Keep in the back of your head that the judge will later instruct the jury that they can find you guilty ONLY if the preponderance of evidence shows that your care fell below the recognized standard of care. If it can be shown that the bad result was due only to an ERROR IN JUDGMENT, this is not sufficient to support a claim of malpractice. After you have "had your say", the plaintiff's lawyer will cross- examine you and try again to discredit your testimony, so don't relax just yet! Remember to keep cool and stick by your testimony. Don't ever waiver or allow him to make you seem unsure. Continue to be polite and patient and continue to make eye contact with the jurors -- after all, your testimony is for them, not for the plaintiff's lawyer!

CLOSING ARGUMENTS:

The witnesses for the defense will all give their testimony after yours, each with the same format of questioning. Hopefully, each of your witnesses is strong and believable in what they say. After every one of them has been heard, first your lawyer will give his summation, or closing argument. The plaintiff's lawyer goes last. Each will do his best to show their case in the best possible light and each will, no doubt, use emotional arguments in an attempt to sway the jury. It is now, totally in the hands of the jurors.

THE JURY IS OUT:

These final minutes or hours are the most emotionally draining. You will wonder what else you could have said or done, but it is all over except for the verdict. In general, the longer the jury takes to reach a decision, the more discord there is among the jurors. They must try to reach a UNANIMOUS decision and also assign the amount of damages (money to be paid if you lose). When they finally come out with their decision, their foreman (a person chosen by them early in the trial) will read the decision to the judge. Win or lose, you are finished!! You are emotionally drained, and probably won't feel much of anything one way or the other except GLAD that it's over. You will vow NEVER to be in court again and may even want to write about your experience. If you are blessed with insight, you will try to discover WHY your patient sued you and make some efforts to change your practice habits so that it doesn't happen again. You might even take risk management seriously!

BIBLIOGRAPHY

1. Rogers, John T: Risk Management in Emergency Medicine: American College Emergency Physicians; 1985

2. Pike vs. Honsinger   155   N.Y. 210, N.E. 760 (1898)

3. Informed Consent: Recall by Patients Tested Postoperatively Robinson, G. and Merav, A. Annals of Thoracic Surgery Vol 22, P3:   Sept   (1976)

4. Unauthorized Treatment - The Doctrine of Informed Consent; Sagall, E.L. and Reed, B.C.; 18 Med. Sci, 67 (1967)

5. Mohr vs. Williams   104 N.W. 12, MN (1905)

6. Schloendorff vs. the Society of New York Hospital, 211 N.Y.; 105 N.E. 92, N.Y. (1914)

7. Natanson vs. Kline, 187 Kans 186; 354 P2d 670; 350 P2d 1093, KS (1960)

8. Cunningham vs. Parikh   472 So 2d 746, Fl. 2 App, P36 (1985)

9. Keane vs. Sloan Kettering Institute for Cancer   Research   464 NYS 2d 548 (1986)

10. King, J.H.   The Law of Medical Practice in a Nutshell,   West Publishing Inc. (1986)

11. Canterbury vs. Spence   150 U.S. APP. DC 263, 464 F 2d 772 (1972)

12. Iowa Code ANN 147.137 (Supp.) (1975)

13. Avoiding Malpractice Liability   Halley, M. Martin, M.D., J.D., FACS;   Bull. Am. Coll. Surg., Vol. 73, Sept. 1988, p5

14. The Importance of Medical Records   228 JAMA, No 1., p118, April 1, 1974

15. James vs. Spear   338 P 2d 22, CA (1959)

16. Rotan vs. Greenbaum   273 F2d 830 (1959)

17.   Snider, Howard C., M.D. Jury of My Peers -- A Surgeon's Encounter with the Malpractice

Crisis   Fountain Press, Montgomery, Ala   1989; ISBN 0-9622607-0-3

18. Danner, Douglas   Medical Malpractice: A Primer for Physicians, The Lawyers Cooperative Publishing Co.   1989   Lib. Cong. Cat. 84-80155

GLOSSARY OF LEGAL TERMS

This glossary is provided to assist you with terms which may possibly be used during a malpractice action.

ABANDONMENT. Failure to fulfill a contract. This is a malpractice charge made when a practitioner stops giving care during the course of a patient's illness, without making arrangements for appropriate continuation and follow-up care.

ABUSE. Excessive or improper use of treatment of something or someone.

ADDITUR. An amount of money added to the jury verdict by the Judge at his discretion to reach a just result, with a new trial as the alternative if the defendant does not agree with the additur.

ADMINISTRATOR. One appointed by a probate court to settle the estate of a decedent.

ADMISSIBILITY (in evidence). Evidence which may be properly introduced in a legal proceeding. The determination as to admissibility is based on legal rules of evidence and is made by the trial judge or a screening panel.

ADMISSION AGAINST INTEREST. A statement made by one person to another in conflict with the interests of the person making the declaration.

ADMISSIONS. Statements by a party which are admissible in evidence as an exception to the hearsay rule. In a malpractice proceeding, an admission would typically be a statement of culpability by the defendant.

AFFIDAVIT. Sworn statement that is usually written.

ALLEGATION. Assertion or claim in the pleadings which states what the plaintiff expects to prove.

ANSWER. A legal document which contains a defendant's written response to a complaint or declaration in a legal proceeding. The answer typically either denies the allegations of the plaintiff or makes new allegations as to why the plaintiff should not recover damages.

APPEAL. The process by which a decision of a lower court is brought for review to a court of higher jurisdiction, typically known as an appellate court.

APPELLATE COURT. The court that reviews trial court decisions. Appellate courts review the transcript of the trial court proceedings and determine whether there were errors of law committed by the trial court.

ARBITRATION. A process whereby a dispute can be settled by a mediator accepted by both parties involved. If the parties have not agreed to follow the decision of the arbitration procedure, the decision is not binding. In some instances, arbitration is used to determine if the case should go to court.

ASSAULT. Intentional and unauthorized act of placing another in apprehension of immediate bodily harm.

ASSUMPTION OF RISK. "Non fit injuria". A party cannot claim damages for an injury caused by a danger which he or she know about, yet voluntarily chose to be exposed to and take the risk that the danger entailed.

AUTHORITATIVE. A person or written work commonly held to be correct. To state that someone or something is authoritative is to implicitly agree with every detail in a specified work. To concur instead only on the accuracy of particular statements of the author or work is to avoid making authorizations beyond your awareness or intent.

BAILIFF. An officer of the court who is in charge of courtroom decorum, directs witnesses to the witness stand, and attends to the jurors.

BILL OF PARTICULARS. Statement defining the details of a claim.

BATTERY. Intentional and unauthorized touching of a person, directly or indirectly, without consent. for example, a surgical procedure performed upon a person without express or implied consent constitutes a battery.

BREACH OF CONTRACT. Failure to act as required by contract. A contract may be implied and initiated when a doctor undertakes the responsibility to treat a patient.

BREACH OF DUTY. Failure to provide the usual standard of care to a patient.

BRIEF. Written statement , prepared by an attorney for a court, that summarizes a case and tells how specific laws are relevant to the case.

BURDEN OF PROOF. In the law of evidence the necessity or duty of affirmatively proving a fact or facts in dispute on an issue raised between the parties in a cause.

CAPTAIN OF THE SHIP. Holds the surgeon in an operation responsible for the negligence of nurses and others working under the direct supervision of that surgeon. Recently, some courts have decided not to uphold this doctrine, and thereby made nurses -- and the hospitals that employ them – liable for their own negligent acts.

CAUSATION. Existence of a connection between the act or omission of the defendant and the injury suffered by the plaintiff. In a suit for negligence, the issue of causation usually requires proof that the plaintiff's harm resulted proximately from the negligence of the defendant.

CAUSE OF ACTION: Set of facts that gives rise to a legal right to redress at law.

CAVEAT. Beware.

COLLATERAL SOURCE. Defendant's payment will not be reduced because the plaintiff has been paid by another source. For example, when one who has won a claim of $100,000 in damages has already received $80,000 in insurance benefits, the defendant physician would still be required to pay the full $100,000.

COMMON LAW. Body of rules and principles based on Anglo-Saxon law, derived from usages and customs, and developed from court decisions based on such law. It is distinguished from statutes enacted by legislatures and all other types of law.

COMPARATIVE NEGLIGENCE. When injuries are judged to be due in part to several different parties, including the plaintiff, the negligence -- and liability -- of each party can be determined on a percentage (comparative) basis.

COMPENSATION. Money payment for damages for the injury sustained proximately by a plaintiff caused by a defendant.

COMPLAINT. The initiatory pleading on the part of the plaintiff in filing a civil lawsuit. Its purpose is to give defendants notice of the general alleged facts constituting the cause of action.

CONFIDENTIAL COMMUNICATION. Information transmitted during the course of a physician-patient relationship.

CONTINGENCY FEE. A fee agreement, between the plaintiff and his attorney, whereby the plaintiff agrees to pay the attorney a percentage of the damages recovered.

CONTRACT. Agreement about what will or will not be done.

CONTRIBUTORY NEGLIGENCE OR COMPARATIVE NEGLIGENCE. Affirmative defense to a successful action against a defendant where the plaintiff's concurrent negligence contributed to his or her own injury, even though the defendant's actions may also have been responsible for the injury.

COUNTERSUIT. Lawsuit brought by the defendant against the plaintiff or plaintiff's attorney. A suit charging the plaintiff with malice would be difficult to prove. Easier to win would be a claim of a poor standard of practice or harassment of the practitioner by the plaintiff's attorney, which would really be a malpractice suit against the attorney.

COURT REPORTER. A professionally trained stenographer who transcribes deposition or trial testimony (and can administer an oath).

DAMAGES. Money receivable through judicial order by a plaintiff sustaining harm, impairment, or loss to his person or property as the result of the accidental, intentional, or negligent act of another. "Compensatory" damages are to compensate the injured party for the injury sustained and nothing more. "Special" damages are the actual out of pocket losses incurred by the plaintiff, such as medical expenses and lost earnings, and are a part of the "compensatory" damages. "Nominal" damages are awarded to demonstrate that a legally cognizable wrong has been committed. "Punitive" damages are awarded to punish a defendant who has acted maliciously or in reckless disregard of the plaintiff's rights.

DEFAMATION. Injury to a person's reputation by acts of libel (writing) or slander (speech).

DEMURRER. Declaration by the defendant stating that even if the accusations made were true, there would be no basis for a suit against the defendant. For example, the claims do not state that the defendant's negligence was a proximate cause of the patient's injury.

DIRECTED VERDICT. The Trial judge may enter a decision, a directed verdict, when a party has failed to present a case with sufficient evidence for jury evaluation.

DISCLOSURE. Divulgence or explaining of information and evidence.

DISCOVERY. Pretrial activities of the parties to litigation to learn of evidence known to the opposing party or various witnesses and therefore to minimize surprises at the time of trial.

DISCOVERY RULE. The statute of limitation starts to run when the patient knows about, or when a diligent patient would have been able to recognize, the negligent act of the practitioner.

DISMISSAL. A legal denial by a court. To dismiss a motion is to deny it; to dismiss an appeal is to affirm the judgment of the trial court.

DISMISSAL WITH PREJUDICE. Legal denial with no right to refile.

DISMISSAL WITHOUT PREJUDICE. Legal denial with preservation of the right to refile.

DUE CARE. Required degree of reasonable or ordinary observation and awareness that a person has and owes to another person by virtue of a special relationship or circumstance. Applicable as a standard of conduct in most personal injury cases but not in medical malpractice cases where the standard is that of the average qualified physician practicing the same specialty as the defendant.

DUE PROCESS. Course of legal proceedings according to those rules and principles which have been established in systems of jurisprudence for the enforcement and protection of private rights. It often means simply a fair hearing.

DUTY. An obligation recognized by the law. A physician's duty to a patient is to provide the degree of care ordinarily exercised by physicians practicing in the came community or area of specialization.

EVIDENCE. All the means by which any alleged matter of fact, the truth of which is submitted to investigation at trial, is established or disproved. Evidence includes the testimony of witnesses, introduction of records, documents, exhibits, objects or any other probative matter offered for the purpose of inducing belief in the party's contention by the judge or jury.

EXPERT WITNESS. Person who has special training, knowledge, skill, or experience in an area relevant to resolution of the legal dispute, that is beyond the average person's knowledge, and who is allowed to offer an opinion as testimony in court.

FIDUCIARY. Person in a position of confidence or trust who undertakes a duty to act for the benefit of another under a given set of circumstances.

HEARSAY. Evidence which does not proceed from the personal knowledge of the witness, but is a repetition of an out-of-court statement and is offered to prove the truth of the matter asserted. The general rule, subject to various exceptions, is that such statements are inadmissible because they rely on the truth and veracity of outside persons not present for cross-examination.

HOSTILE WITNESS. A witness whose position or viewpoint is adverse to that of the attorney who called him or her to the stand.

HYPOTHETICAL QUESTION.   A form of question put to a witness, usually an expert witness, in which things which counsel claims are or will be proved are stated as a factual supposition and the witness is asked to respond, state or explain the conclusion based on the assumptions and question.

INFORMED CONSENT.   Patient's voluntary agreement to accept treatment based upon the patient's awareness of the nature of his or her disease, the material risks and benefits of the proposed treatment, the alternative treatments and risks, or the choice of no treatment at all (and the risk of that alternative).

INTERROGATORIES.   A written list of questions given to witnesses or defendants to obtain information that would be difficult to obtain from memory at deposition.

JOINT AND SEVERAL LIABILITY.   In cases where the plaintiff is to some degree responsible for the injury or damages claimed, the trier of fact may apportion damages according to fault among the defendants whose degree of fault is greater than the injured person.   Damages shall not be a joint liability and shall not be subject to any right of contribution. Sometimes the entire liability will be imposed upon a single one of several defendants (such as the only one who can pay-- the "deep pocket").

JUDICIAL MODIFICATION OF AWARDS.   If a jury award is clearly so inadequate or excessive as to be inconsistent with the preponderance of the evidence, the trial court may order a new trial relative to damages only, or the judge may condition the grant of a new trial upon any party's refusal to accept an amount determined by the trial court.

LIMITED IMMUNITY FOR NON-PROFIT DIRECTORS.   Civil immunity is provided for members, directors, or trustees serving with or without compensation, and to officers serving without compensation at non-profit hospitals, charitable organizations, and governmental entities, when they act in good faith.   This provision does not apply in cases of willful or wanton misconduct.

LIMITED MEDICAL IMMUNITY.   Physicians, nurses and dentists shall have limited immunity from liability when their services are rendered voluntarily, without either expectation or receipt of compensation, at the request of a hospital, public school, non-profit organization or agency of the state or its political subdivisions.   Similar immunity is provided to hospitals, public schools, non-profit, organizations and agencies of the state and its political subdivisions when they participate in providing medical services with no expectation or realization of compensation.   This provision does not apply in cases involving gross negligence or willful or wanton misconduct.

LOSS OF CONSORTIUM. Loss of affection, companionship, sex, and other benefits when a spouse or other close person dies or is severely injured. Payment for such loss is often sought in malpractice claims.

MALICE. The performance of a wrongful act without just cause or excuse, with an intent to inflict an injury, or under such circumstances that the law will imply an evil intent.

MALICIOUS PROSECUTION. A difficult to prove counterclaim that a lawsuit has been brought without probable cause and with malicious intent.

MALPRACTICE. Negligence or misconduct on the part of a healthcare practitioner, lawyer, or other professional that causes injury and leads to a civil suit. Failure to use the degree of skill and knowledge exhibited by other professionals in similar circumstances is usually involved in the claim.

MATERIAL. Influential and of necessary effect. Having to do with substance, as distinguished from form.

MENTAL ANGUISH. Pain, fear, and anxiety that follows a damaging or endangering physical or mental injury or loss.

MERITORIOUS. Legally proper and deserving.

NEGLIGENCE. Failure to act as a reasonable, prudent person would under similar circumstances.

PAIN AND SUFFERING. All intangible damages, including discomfort and mental distress.

PATIENT PRIVILEGE. Right of a patient to have information disclosed to a practitioner kept secret. This right is usually waived in court when the patient sues the practitioner.

PRIMA FACIE EVIDENCE. That which seems to be correct and will be accepted by the court as fact if not contradicted in rebuttal by other evidence.

PROFESSIONAL AFFIDAVIT. In cases of professional malpractice, the defendant must file an affidavit from an expert that at least one negligent act has occurred. If the period of limitation will expire within 10 days of the filing, the plaintiff shall have 45 days to provide the affidavit. The defendant is given 30 days from the point of the affidavit's filing to respond.

p.p.a. Abbreviation for "per pro ami" or "by next friend." A minor plaintiff's action is brought by his or her representative, usually by his or her mother or father as next friend.

PRIVILEGED COMMUNICATION. Communication made within a certain trust relationship, such as from patient to physician, which is privileged in the sense that the person making the communication may be statutorily granted the qualified power to prevent the other from divulging the nature of the communication in court. A physician has a legal duty not to disclose to unauthorized persons the patient's confidential information.

PROXIMATE CAUSE. Act of commission or omission that through an uninterrupted sequence of events directly results in an injury that otherwise would not have occurred, or else becomes a substantial factor in causing an injury.

REASONABLE PERSON. Hypothetical person used as an objective test or standard against which a defendant's conduct in a negligence action will be judged. Not the standard for professional negligence in a medical malpractice action which requires expert opinion that the defendant doctor failed to comply with the standard of the average qualified physician in the same medical specialty.

REMAND. To hold over for future deliberations. To send a case back for further consideration.

REMITTITUR. Order by a judge for a plaintiff to remit (give back) part of an unreasonably large award.

REMOTE POSSIBILITY. A legal consideration that an event carried less than a 50% plus chance of determining outcome.

RES IPSA LOQUITUR. "The thing speaks for itself." Means of proving negligence which depends on the fact, obvious to any lay person, that the injury would not have occurred in the absence of negligence. No expert witness is required to present complex arguments or facts proving guilt.

RES JUDICATA or RES ASJUDICATA. "The matter judged." Decided by previous lawsuits whose precedents will be followed.

RESPONDEAT SUPERIOR. "Let the master answer." The employer (master) is responsible for the actions of employees (servants).

STANDARD OF CARE. Measure against which a defendant's conduct is compared. The required standard in a professional negligence or medical malpractice case is the standard of the average qualified practitioner in the same area of medical specialization under the same or similar circumstances.

STARE DECISIS. "Let the decision stand." Follow previous court decisions on similar matters.

STATUTE OF LIMITATION FOR MEDICAL MALPRACTICE. The time within which a suit must be filed after recognizing the injury, usually two to three years. Persons who are legally incompetent because of mental retardation or mental illness and minors who are five years or older shall be subject to a two-year period of limitation for medical malpractice actions. For minors under the age of five, the two-year period of limitation for medical malpractice shall begin upon the child's fifth birthday. The statute of response for those who are legally incompetent because of mental retardation or mental illness and for minors who are five years or older shall be five years from the date that the negligent or wrongful act occurred. When a minor under the age of five is the victim of a wrongful or negligent medical act, action may be brought anytime before the child's 10th birthday.

STIPULATION. An agreement entered into between opposing counsel in a pending action.

SUBPOENA DUCES TECUM. A court order that requires a person to personally bring to the court proceeding a specified document or property in his or her possession or under his or her control.

SUBROGATION. Substitution of one party for another (e.g., an insurance company may sue someone if the client had the right to sue).

SUMMARY JUDGMENT. Court decision based on the belief that there is no significant evidence or basis in law to support a claim for damages.

SUMMATIONS. Talks to the jury near the end of a trial in which each attorney, and sometimes the judge, reviews the main points of the case.

SUPERSEDEAS BOND. Money that must be paid by a defendant who is appealing a judgment. Even though an award for damages has been appealed, a fee (the supersedeas bond) must be paid by the defendant until the final judgment has been made.

TORT. A civil wrong other than a breach of contract.

TORTFEASOR. A party who commits a tort, a legal violation.

VICARIOUS LIABILITY. Derivative or secondary liability predicated not upon direct fault, but by virtue of the defendant's relationship to the actual wrongdoer, in which the former is presumed to hold a position of responsibility and control over the latter.

VOIR DIRE. "To speak the truth." The process of questioning and choosing jurors.

WAIVER. Intentional and volitional renunciation of a known claim or right, or a failure to avail oneself of a possible advantage to be derived from another's act. for example, a waiver might allow a person to testify to information that would ordinarily be protected as a privileged communication.

WANTON. Malicious, immoral, or reckless conduct that evinces a disregard for the consequences or for the rights or safety of others.

WILFUL. Term descriptive of conduct that encompasses the continuum from intentional to reckless.

WRONGFUL DEATH. Statute allowing that the death of a person may be grounds for a civil suit.

WRONGFUL LIFE. Lawsuit that charges a health practitioner with being responsible for the life (undesired birth) of an individual (e.g., following an unsuccessful sterilization or failure to give genetic counseling).

EXAMINATION RISK MANAGEMENT COURSE

1. What is the reason for the current malpractice crisis?

    (a) Bad doctors

    (b) Too many lawyers

    (c) Insurance company premium increases

    (d) All of the above

2. What is the definition of risk management?

    (a) Technique of preventing malpractice

    (b) The science of injury prevention

    (c) Technique for prevention of lawsuits

    (d) The practice of prevention of injury due to hazardous conditions in the workplace

3. Our legal system is best described as:

    (a) Corrupt

    (b) Unresponsive to changing mores

    (c) Expensive

    (d) Adversarial

4. When does a physician-patient contract occur?

    (a) When the consent form is signed

    (b) When the patient agrees to the treatment plan

(c) As soon as the doctor examines the patient

(d) a and b

5. What constitutes medical malpractice?

(a) Negligence in providing medical care

(b) Injury to a patent resulting from medical care

(c) A valid physician-patient relationship

(d) All of the above

6. What is proximate cause?

(a) A course of action causing an untoward result; precipitating a condition; or aggravating a condition

(b) A condition arising from excessive closeness

(c) The cause of a malpractice claim

(d) Something only a lawyer would look for

7. Why do patients resort to legal action against doctors?

(a) Malpractice has occurred

(b) The patient is angry at the doctor

(C) Advised to do so by friends or family

(d) Unrealistic expectations of treatment (not fulfilled)

(e) All of the above

8. What types of malpractice insurance are generally available?

(a) Expensive and ridiculously expensive

(b) Claims-made and occurrence

(c) Claims-made and modified claims-made

(d) Occurrence and non-occurrence

9. What is a tail?

   (a) Coverage that must be purchased when canceling a clams- made policy

   (b) Coverage that must be purchased when canceling an occurrence policy

   (C) Coverage that usually costs three times the first year claims-made rate

   (d) a and c

10. Are punitive damages covered by malpractice insurance?

    (a) Yes

    (b) No

11. Is the conduct of physician's employees relevant to the patient's feelings about the doctor?

    (a) Yes

    (b) No

12. Can a doctor release medical information about a patient to another doctor without the patient's consent?

    (a) Yes

    (b) No

    (C) Yes, in cases of Workman's Compensation

    (d) b and c

13. Abandonment can be charged for the failure of a doctor to:

    (a) Follow up treatment on a patient

    (b) See a patient in the hospital in a timely manner

    (C) Notify a patient of a missed appointment

    (d) All of the above

14. Informed consent is:

    (a) Proved when the patient signs the consent form

    (b) Obtained through complete risk disclosure by the physician

    (C) Often obtained through written and audiovisual material

    (d) all of the above

    (e) b and c only

15. What is significant about "Mohr vs. Williams"?

    (a) First modern case dealing with informed consent

    (b) First malpractice suit in USA

    (C) First multimillion-dollar award in USA

    (d) Nothing

16. Does a signed hospital consent form serve to protect the physician against charges of "lack of informed consent"?

    (a) Yes, in most all states

    (b) No

    (C) Yes, but only in a few states

17. A patient's recall of preoperative discussion concerning risks and benefits is:

   (a) Usually considerable

   (b) Better with audiovisual materials than when given by the doctor

   (C) Usually no better than 30%

   (d) Usually better than 50%

18. What is the best method to document informed consent?

   (a) Consent form

   (b) Video or audio taping of information session

   (C) Writing in the patient's chart by the doctor that the information was given

   (d) Having the patent write and sign that adequate information was given

   (e) all of the above

19. How do you handle the patient who refuses to listen to the risks of treatment and wants the doctor to "do what you think is best"?

   (a) Refuse to treat

   (b) Refer to another physician

   (C) Make them listen

   (d) Have the patient write in the chart that they do not wish to have the risks of the procedure disclosed and that they want to proceed with the recommended treatment.

20. Why is documentation n the medical chart essential?

   (a) It provides an adequate summary of the patient's condition, course of treatment, and response to therapy

   (b) It fulfills a JCAH requirement

   (C) It keeps people employed in the medical records room

(d) It is the only proof of the adequacy of medical care in a malpractice action

(e) All of the above

21. What is the best way to alter a medical record?

    (a) A line through the incorrect entry; a corrected entry dated and signed

    (b) Erase the incorrect entry neatly and make a new entry

    (C) Tear out the page and start over again

    (d) All of the above

22. In a malpractice action the jury will be more likely to believe:

    (a) The physician who has "perfect recall" of an event that is not documented in the chart

    (b) The plaintiff who has "perfect recall" of the event

    (C) The lawyer who wears a 3-piece suit

    (d) The lawyer who speaks more eloquently

23. Under what circumstances is a patient entitled to the information in his/her medical record?

    (a) Only after the bill is pad

    (b) Only after obtaining a court order

    (C) Upon request

    (d) Never, as it contains sensitive medical information

24. Can a patient's medical record be furnished to any third party upon demand?

    (a) Never

    (b) Always

(C)   Only with the express written permission of the patient

(d)   Without the patient's permission in some cases of private insurance and Workman's Compensation

(e)   c and d

25.   Under what circumstances should the medical record be (properly) altered?

(a)   Upon receipt of an "intent to sue" letter

(b)   Upon careful review of the chart, just before trial

(C)   During the course of medical treatment upon finding an obvious error, or mis-entry

(d) Never

26.   What details should be documented in the patient's record?

(a)   Only those details directly related to medical events

(b)   all events of significance to patient care as well as compliance and attitude of the patient, as these could relate to the course of treatment

(C)   All events of significance including disagreements with others care or comments

(d)   As little as possible — to confuse lawyers

27.   What is an "incident"?

(a)   A disgruntled patient who complains about the bill 4w

(b)   A complication occurring after medical care

(C)   A patient receiving the wrong prescription

(d)   All of the above

28.   Why should incidents be promptly reported to your malpractice

insurance carrier?

    (a) So they may set up a preliminary investigation prior to any suit being filed

    (b)   So potential losses can be estimated and money held aside in a "reserve account"

    (C)   Reporting incidents makes the doctor more introspective and claims-conscious

    (d)   All of the above

29.   When should an incident be reported?

    (a)   As soon as possible by return-receipt mail

    (b)   Once a month by telephone

    (C)   Weekly by FAX

    (d)   After receiving an "intent to sue" letter

30.   When you receive official notice of a suit, you should:

    (a)   Notify your malpractice carrier

    (b)   Send all legal documents after copying, to the malpractice carrier

    (C)   Record your recollections of the case

    (d)   Copy and safeguard the medical record

    (e)   All of the above

31.   What is a deposition?

    (a)   A pre-trial "fishing expedition" for information to be used at trial

    (b)   A boring and tedious process whereby the deponent is often "tested" by the plaintiff's attorney to see how he/she will react at trial

    (c)   An official question and answer session, which can and will be used at trial

(d) All of the above

32. A settlement offer

    (a) Is always a sign of weakness

    (b) Is often a logical recourse

    (c) Is not an admission of guilt

    (d) All of the above

    (e) b and c

33. Most people file lawsuits because of

    (a) An unanticipated event or expense

    (b) Advice of friends or relatives

    (c) Anger

    (d) All of the above

34. When you first discover a "medical incident' you should

    (a) Notify your insurance company

    (b) Call your lawyer

    (c) Dismiss the patent from your practice

    (d) Dictate a lengthy note in the patient's chart

35. When you receive a "letter of intent' to sue, you should

    (a) Notify your malpractice carrier

    (b) Send the original legal papers to the insurance company and keep copies for your records

(c) Make 4 copies of the patient records and pace the original SEALED in a safe

(d) All of the above

36. In a malpractice suit, do you need your own defense attorney?

(a) Yes

(b) No

(c) Usually only to protect you if the claim is above your policy limits

(d) Only if you don't trust the lawyer chosen by the insurance company

37. An Interrogatory is

(a) An informal question and answer session in front of a court reporter

(b) A question asked by a lawyer in court

(c) A questionnaire sent to accumulate basic facts

(d) A formalized method of selecting jury members

38. A Deposition is

(a) A semiformal examination whose answers can be used in court

(b) A chance for the opposing attorney to "size you up"

(c) A chance for you to show off your knowledge

(d) a and b

39. What is an "authoritative source" in the legal sense?

(a) A source (book, journal, etc.) which is generally held in esteem by most people

(b) An article or book written by a respected author

(c) A source, if accepted as "authoritative", that must be accepted in its entirety, even if you disagree with some portions of the source

(d) all of the above

40. Why is it sometimes wise to offer to settle a case?

    (a) It reduces the uncertainty of a trial verdict

    (b) It causes less emotional duress

    (c) It is less costly than a trial

    (d) All of the above

41 What is the voir dire?

    (a) The position held by the jury foreman

    (b) A procedure used by the judge prior to sentencing

    (c) The process of jury selection

    (d) The process of pretrial discovery

42. In the voir dire, each lawyer may

    (a) attempt to assess the prejudices of a potential juror

    (b) use "strikes" to remove a troublesome potential juror

    (c) use a psychologist to get a profile on juror

    (d) all of the above

43. A person who sincerely believes that a trial is a search for the truth

    (a) Is naive

    (b) Will be sorely disappointed

(c) Has probably never been to a trial

(d) All of the above

44. A lawyer can "lead the witness" during the

    (a) Direct examination

    (b) Cross-examination

    (c) trial at all times

    (d) trial at no time

45. Juries will usually

    (a) Try to believe the doctor if his case is well-documented
    (b) Put more credence in the plaintiffs "total recall'

    (c) Be more forgiving for bad behavior of the plaintiff than the doctor

    (d) All of the above

46. The opening statement and closing arguments

    (a) Are made by both defense and plaintiff's lawyers

    (b) Do not necessarily contain factual information

    (c) Show off the lawyer's oratorical or theatrical prowess

    (d) All of the above

47. The closing argument

    (a) Is made by both attorneys

    (b) Is made only by the defense attorney

    (c) Is made only by the plaintiffs attorney

(d) Is usually unconvincing

48. The jury's verdict must

(a) Always be unanimous

(b) Represent a majority

(c) Be read by the bailiff

(d) Always be fair to both parties

49. In a malpractice trial

(a) The jury verdict, if for the plaintiff, does not include the amount of the award

(b) The jury verdict, if for the defense, must penalize the plaintiff

(c) The jury verdict, if for the plaintiff, must also include the amount of the award

(d) None of the above

EXAMINATION RISK MANAGEMENT COURSE
ANSWER SHEET

1. What is the reason for the current malpractice crisis?

    Bad doctors

    Too many lawyers

    Insurance company premium increases

    (d) All of the above

2. What is the definition of risk management?

    (c) Technique for prevention of lawsuits

3. Our legal system is best described as:

    (d) Adversarial

4. When does a physician-patient contract occur?

    (b) When the patient agrees to the treatment plan

5. What constitutes medical malpractice?

    Negligence in providing medical care

    Injury to a patient resulting from medical care

    A valid physician-patient relationship

    (d) All of the above

6. What is proximate cause?

 (a) A course of action causing an untoward result; precipitating a condition; or aggravating a condition

7. Why do patients resort to legal action against doctors?

 Malpractice has occurred

 The patient is angry at the doctor

 Advised to do so by friends or family

 Unrealistic expectations of treatment (not fulfilled)

 (e) All of tie above

8. What types of malpractice insurance are generally available?

 (b) Claims-made and occurrence

9. What is a tail?

 Coverage that must be purchased when canceling a claims-made policy

 Coverage that usually costs three times the first year claims-made rate

 (d) a and c

10. Are punitive damages covered by malpractice insurance?

 (b) No

11. Is the conduct of physician's employees relevant to the patient's feelings about the doctor?

 (a) Yes

12. Can a doctor release medical information about a patient to another doctor without the patient's consent?

   No

   Yes, in cases of Workman's Compensation

   (d)　b and c

13. Abandonment can be charged for the failure of a doctor to:

   Follow up treatment on a patient

   See a patient in the hospital in a timely manner

   Notify a patient of a missed appointment

   (d)　All of the above

14. Informed consent is:

   Obtained through complete risk disclosure by the physician

   Often obtained through written and audiovisual material

   (e)　b and c only

15. What is significant about "Mohr vs. Williams"?

   (a)　First modern case dealing with informed consent

16. Does a signed hospital consent form serve to protect the physician against charges of lack of informed consent"?

   (c)　Yes, but only in a few states

17. A patient's recall of preoperative discussion concerning risks and benefits is:

    (c)   Usually no better than 30%

18. What is the best method to document informed consent?

    Consent form

    Video or audio taping of information session

    Writing in the patent's chart by the doctor that the information was given

    Having the patent write and sign that adequate information was given

    (e) all of the above

19. How do you handle the patient who refuses to listen to the risks of treatment and wants the doctor to "do what you think is best"?

    (d)   Have the patient write n the chart that they do not wish to have the risks of the procedure disclosed and that they want to proceed with the recommended treatment.

20. Why is documentation in the medical chart essential?

    It provides an adequate summary of the patient's condition, course of treatment, and

    Response to therapy

    It fulfills a JCAH requirement

    It keeps people employed in the medical records room

    It is the only proof of the adequacy of medical care in a malpractice   action

    (e) All of the above

21. What is the best way to alter a medical record"

    (a) A line through the incorrect entry; a corrected entry dated and signed

22. In a malpractice action the jury will be more likely to believe:

    (b) The plaintiff who has "perfect recall" of the event

23. Under what circumstances is a patient entitled to the information in his/her medical record?

    (c) Upon request

24. Can a patient's medical record be furnished to any third party upon demand?

    Only with the express written permission of the patient

    Without the patient's permission in some cases of private insurance and Workman's Compensation

    (e) c and d

25. Under what circumstances should the medical record be (properly) altered?

    (c) During the course of medical treatment upon finding an obvious error, or mis-entry

26. What details should be documented in the patient's record?

    (b) All events of significance to patient care as well as compliance and attitude of the patient, as these could relate to the course of treatment

29. When should an incident be reported?

    (a) As soon as possible by return-receipt mail

27. What is an "incident"?

    A disgruntled patient who complains about the bill

    A complication occurring after medical care

    A patient receiving the wrong prescription.

    (d) All of the above

28. Why should incidents be promptly reported to your malpractice insurance carrier?

    So they may set up a preliminary investigation prior to any suit being filed

    So potential losses can be estimated and money held aside in a "reserve account"

    Reporting incidents makes the doctor more introspective and claims-conscious

    (d) All of the above

30. When you receive official notice of a suit, you should:

    Notify your malpractice carrier

    Send all legal documents after copying, to the malpractice carrier

    Record your recollections of the case

    Copy and safeguard the medical record

    (e) All of the above

31. What is a deposition?

A pre-trial "fishing expedition' for information to be used at trial

A boring and tedious process whereby the deponent is often "tested" by the plaintiffs attorney to see how he/she will react at trial

An official question and answer session which can and will be used at trial

(d) All of the above

32. A settlement offer Is often a logical recourse

Is not an admission of guilt

(a)   b and c

33. Most people file lawsuits because of

An unanticipated event or expense

Advice of friends or relatives

Anger

(d)   All of the above

34. When you first discover a "medical incident" you should

(a) Notify your insurance company

35. When you receive a "letter of intent" to sue, you should

Notify your malpractice carrier

Send the original legal papers to the insurance company and keep copies for your records

Make 4 copies of the patient records and place the original SEALED in a safe

(d) All of the above

36. In a malpractice suit, do you need your own defense attorney?

(c) Usually only to protect you if the claim is above your policy limits

37. An Interrogatory is

(c) A questionnaire sent to accumulate basic facts

38. A Deposition is

A semiformal examination whose answers can be used in court A

chance for the opposing attorney to "size you up"

(d) a and b

39. What is an "authoritative source" in the legal-sense?

(c) A source, if accepted as "authoritative", that must be accepted in its entirety, even if you disagree with some portions of the source

40. Why is it sometimes wise to offer to "settle" a case?

It reduces the uncertainty of a trial verdict

It causes less emotional duress

It is less costly than a trial

(d) All of the above

41. What is the voir dire?

(c) The process of jury selection

42. In the voir dire, each lawyer may

attempt to assess the prejudices of a potential juror use "strikes" to remove a troublesome potential juror use a psychologist to get a profile on jurors

(e) all of the above

43. A person who sincerely believes that a trial is a search for the truth

Is naive

Will be sorely disappointed

Has probably never been to a trial

(d) All of the above

44. A lawyer can "lead the witness" during the

(b) Cross-examination

45. Juries will usually

Try to believe the doctor if his case is well-documented

Put more credence in the plaintiff's "total recall"

Be more forgiving for bad behavior of the plaintiff than the doctor

(d) All of the above

46. The opening statement and closing arguments

Are made by both defense and plaintiff's lawyers

Do not necessarily contain factual information

Show off the lawyer's oratorical or theatrical prowess

    (d)   All of the above

47.   The closing argument

    (a)   Is made by both attorneys

48.   The jury's verdict must

    (a)   Always be unanimous

49.   In a malpractice trial

    (c)   The jury verdict, if for the plaintiff, must also include the amount of the award

www.ingramcontent.com/pod-product-compliance
Lightning Source LLC
Chambersburg PA
CBHW081210180526
45170CB00006B/2290